THE

Career Guide

THE
FBI
Career Guide

Inside Information on Getting Chosen for and Succeeding in
One of the Toughest, Most Prestigious Jobs in the World

Joseph W. Koletar

AMACOM

American Management Association

New York • Atlanta • Brussels • Chicago • Mexico City • San Francisco
Shanghai • Tokyo • Toronto • Washington, D.C.

Special discounts on bulk quantities of AMACOM books are available to corporations, professional associations, and other organizations. For details, contact Special Sales Department, AMACOM, a division of American Management Association, 1601 Broadway, New York, NY 10019.
Tel.: 212-903-8316. Fax: 212-903-8083.
Web site: www.amacombooks.org

This publication is designed to provide accurate and authoritative information in regard to the subject matter covered. It is sold with the understanding that the publisher is not engaged in rendering legal, accounting, or other professional service. If legal advice or other expert assistance is required, the services of a competent professional person should be sought.

Library of Congress Cataloging-in-Publication Data

Koletar, Joseph W.
        The FBI career guide : inside information on getting chosen for and succeeding in one of the toughest, most prestigious jobs in the world / Joseph W. Koletar.
        p. cm.
    Includes index.
    ISBN-10: 0-8144-7317-2
    ISBN-13: 978-0-8144-7317-7
    1. United States. Federal Bureau of Investigation—Vocational guidance.   2. United States Federal Bureau of Investigation—Officials and employees.   I. Title.

HV8144.F43K65   2006
363.25023'73—dc22

2006004763

Printing number

HB 09.20.2019

In memory of Second Lieutenant Joseph R. Natoli,
of Clearfield, Pennsylvania; Military Intelligence,
1st Infantry Division, United States Army,
Republic of Vietnam, July 29, 1967.

A fellow Penn Stater and fallen warrior,
who was in the wrong place at the wrong time,
but for the right reasons.

May you rest in peace.

Contents

Contents

Preface

This book is about a seeming paradox called the Federal Bureau of Investigation. It is at once one of the most familiar and least known entities in the world. Many people think they "know" the FBI from books, television, newspapers, and the movies. But they know only bits and pieces, and many of these are wrong, owing to the artistic license writers' and directors' take in producing works of fiction. The real FBI is exciting enough, and it is much more complex and intriguing than even the most adventurous work of fiction can depict. I know; I spent the majority of my adult life in it.

Before I began writing this book, both I and my editor, Ellen Kadin, spent considerable time thinking about whether there was even a need for a book like this. At first glance there seemed to be a number of "how to" books on the market about applying for federal investigative jobs, and even a few that concentrated on the FBI. With time, however, we realized there was a gaping hole in the available literature. None of these books presented a picture of what New Agents Training was like. None, to our knowledge, shared the insights of Special Agents involved in recruiting, processing, and training new agents. And none of these books described what the job was about—about how it felt, how it smelled and tasted. Its good parts and its bad parts. In short, an inside view. Thus, this book was born.

This book explains the application process and training program for new agents, but it goes far beyond these essentials to discuss what it is like to be an FBI Agent—the routine duties, typical field office assignments, specialty programs, and foreign assignments; the career development program; the effect of the job on one's self and family; and the life after a career with the Bureau. It also deals with the incorrect assumptions applicants often have and the common mistakes they make.

But rather than dwell on the negative, this book offers tips and suggestions as to how to make yourself a more attractive candidate for one of the most sought-after jobs in the world. For example, in the three years following the events of 9/11, the FBI hired 2,200 Special Agents. Actually, 150,000 people applied. That is a hiring ratio of 68 to 1. This book will help you stand out in that group of 68 other competitors who want the same job as you do. There are no guarantees that you will make it. Indeed, after reading this book you may decide that the position of Special Agent is not for you—and that is fine, too. Too many people waste precious time and money trying to qualify for a position that they may never be able to get or may be unhappy with once they do get it. Better to find these things out sooner rather than later. For others, this book will whet your appetite for excitement, since the real FBI is much more thrilling and tempting as an employer than you could possibly have imagined. To all of you, I wish good luck.

This book was possible because I spent 25 years as an FBI Agent and senior executive. Starting in my first office, Miami, in the late sixties, through my duties as a Section Chief in the Criminal Investigative Division, I served in two field offices, one Resident Agency, three FBI Headquarters Divisions, and the Office of the Director. During that time I investigated bank robberies, police killings, and kidnappings; I testified at over 50 criminal proceedings; I banged up more than a few FBI cars and ran auto theft and bomb squads; I got my picture on the front page of the *New York Times* and the entire back page of the *New York Daily News*; I testified before Congress, performed congressional liaison duties, and drafted hundreds of position papers and policy memoranda. I also commanded the FBI "air force" of 300 pilots and 97 aircraft, served as a counselor to the FBI National

Academy, attended the Program for Senior Managers in Government at Harvard University, and was the U.S. representative to the Senior Executive Officers Course at the Australian Police Staff College. Similarly, I was in charge of formulating and executing a $2.5 billion budget; I directed a Sexual Exploitation of Children Task Force, was the number-three executive in the FBI's largest field office (New York City), and helped plan the centennial celebration of the Statue of Liberty. I supervised White House Background Investigations, was involved in cases that spawned three movies, and ran the FBI's Witness Protection Program. I also got dinged a few times for screw-ups, some of which were my fault and some not. As the noted author Joseph Heller has said, "So it goes."

If that seems like a lot to do in a 25-year career that started under the legendary J. Edgar Hoover, it is not, for the FBI is a dynamic and complex place. For the smart and ambitious, it is a huge canvas upon which one can paint a career in thousands of colors. It is a demanding career, but it is rewarding—sometimes wildly so.

I am the son of a Pennsylvania coal miner who had to drop out of the eighth grade to support his widowed mother and six siblings. For his entire adult life my father had to labor at jobs that were well below his intellect and capabilities because he never had the chance, in the early 1900s, to finish his education. In contrast, I found myself, at age 30, reading *Miranda* rights to a sitting vice president of the United States. Later, I was saluted by Marine guards as I entered the White House. Only the FBI can do that.

A career with the FBI is an adventure and a journey, sometimes with almost magical powers. But it can also be a demanding mistress. A friend of mine best summed it up at the party to celebrate his departure from the FBI. Referring to his career in the Bureau, he said: "It filled my soul, and it broke my heart."

A demanding mistress, indeed; but one with great beauty and allure. Let's meet the lady.

Acknowledgments

Every book is a journey, full of surprises, bumps, and unexpected turns. Completing that journey would not be possible without the help of many people, some near and some far away. This work is no exception.

While any mistakes or omissions are my sole responsibility, the following friends and associates were of invaluable assistance:

First, my thanks to my friend Hank Kennedy, president of AMA-COM, the publishing arm of the American Management Association, for suggesting this book and, also, for many eventful lunches.

Second, to my editor, Ellen Kadin, whose persistence was in no small part responsible for this work seeing the light of day. May her New York Mets someday see the light at the end of the tunnel.

Third, to my wife, Martha, and daughter, Lauren, for putting up with a disorganized author.

Finally, to the men and women of the FBI, especially those with whom I served. In particular, to the members of Bank Robbery Squads 22 and 221 in the New York Office, circa 1970–1975. Especially to Goober, who saved my life. No finer group of human beings ever existed. Bank robberies, terrorism, kidnappings, bombings, fugitives, hijackings—we did it all. Thank you for teaching me my trade and for helping me learn to love an institution.

Others were also instrumental in my completing this effort, in particular: the unknown and, unfortunately, unnamed assistant directors at FBI Headquarters who saw some merit in this project and approved it; Public Affairs Specialist Neal Schiff, of the FBI's Office of Public Affairs; Public Affairs Specialist Kurt Crawford, of the FBI Academy; Supervisory Special Agent Joe Carrico, of the Special Agent Selection Unit at FBI Headquarters; Supervisory Special Agent Mike Esposito, of the New Agents Training Unit at Quantico; Professor Edwin Delattre of Boston University; Professor John Kramer of The Pennsylvania State University; Supervisory Special Agent Bill Calla- han, of the Applicant Squad in the FBI's New York Office; retired Special Agent "Down Town" Kenny Brown, who reads very slowly; former Assistant Special Agent in Charge Jim Murphy, whose words I purloined; Special Agent Glen Bartolomei; Special Agent James T. "Tim" Screen, of the Applicant Squad in the New York Office; and retired Special Agent Mike Griffin, former applicant coordinator of the Columbia, South Carolina, office. Many thanks, guys.

THE
FBI
Career Guide

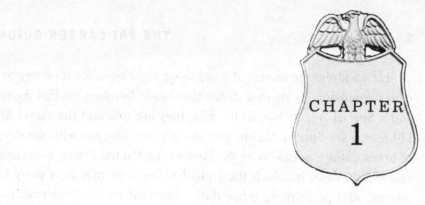

What Is the FBI?

It is said that Google and Starbucks are possibly the two most recognized brands in the world. That may be true, but the FBI is not too far behind them. As a result of almost eighty years of books, movies, TV shows, and news media coverage, the FBI is probably the best-known governmental entity on the face of the earth. Yet, for all its visibility, the FBI remains a thing of mystery, of intrigue, and to some, of fear and suspicion.

Being part of the FBI, especially being an FBI Agent, is not for everyone. The mental, physical, emotional, social, and economic challenges of this work can deter many potential applicants. It is, however, an achievement that defines a large part of a person's life, even if he or she does not stay until retirement. Having been an agent will forever set you apart from most of the rest of the world; and it will be seen as a significant, if not the most significant, characteristic of your personal and professional life. In many ways, the Special Agent designation is a magnifying glass. It enhances the positive and accentuates the negative. In short, if the FBI as an institution is a brand, its members are branded, especially those who occupy the premier position, that of being a Special Agent.

Let's address the matter of word usage right now, for it often generates confusion. Is there a distinction made between an FBI Agent and a Special Agent? No, in the FBI, they are one and the same. All FBI agents are Special Agents, and as such are "charged with the duty of investigating violations of the laws of the United States, collecting evidence in cases in which the United States is or may be a party in interest, and performing other duties imposed by law." So read the credentials each Special Agent is issued upon graduation from New Agents Training. The technical, legal name of the position is Special Agent, but that term is used mainly in courtrooms and written materials. FBI agents refer to each other as "agents," never as "Special Agents," as in "She's an agent in Chicago."

So, too, with the FBI's name. The FBI is often referred to as "the Bureau," as if no other bureaus existed within the federal government. Within the FBI, the term "the Bureau" is used in two ways. It can be a reference to the entire FBI, as in "I joined the Bureau in 1986," or it can refer to FBI Headquarters, as in "The Bureau is coming out with a new transfer policy."

The FBI that we know today is the principal investigative arm of the U.S. Department of Justice. Although it is one of 32 federal law enforcement agencies, it is perhaps the best known. The FBI is charged with investigating specific crimes assigned to it and also with providing the greater law enforcement community with a range of supporting services. The authority of the FBI comes from a series of congressional statutes, among them Title 28 United States Code, Section 533, which authorizes the attorney general to appoint officials to detect and prosecute crimes against the United States; Title 18 United States Code, Section 3052, which authorizes FBI agents to make arrests, serve warrants, and carry firearms; Title 18 United States Code, Section 3107, which authorizes FBI agents to make seizures under warrant; and Title 28 Code of Federal Regulations, Section 0.85, which outlines the responsibilities of the FBI with regard to supporting other law enforcement agencies.

The Development of the FBI

For all its fame and, some would say, notoriety, the FBI began as a function with no formal name. Founded on July 26, 1908, as a team within the U.S. Department of Justice, what is now the FBI was first a workforce of 34 agents established by Attorney General Charles Bonaparte during the presidency of Theodore Roosevelt. Roosevelt had earlier served as Civil Service Commissioner (1889–1895); civil service functions had long been dominated by politics rather than professionalism, so during his tenure, Roosevelt and many other progressives such as Bonaparte believed serious reforms were needed. Investigators assigned to the group that would become the FBI were referred to as members of the "Special Agent force"; many were former detectives and Secret Service Agents. The latter came from an agency that had been in existence for almost half a century. Indeed, the U.S. Secret Service was formed in 1865, to suppress the rampant counterfeiting of currency during the Civil War. That Secret Service Agents should have a role in the early stage of the FBI was logical, since as late as 1907 the attorney general had to call on Secret Service "operatives" to conduct investigations because he lacked an investigative force of his own.

The Early Years

When the first Special Agent force was established, there were few federal crimes to investigate and so those early investigators worked mainly on banking, bankruptcy, antitrust, and land-fraud crimes. Since there was no training program, a premium was placed on hiring persons with prior law enforcement or legal training. A little less than six months later, the Special Agent force acquired its first formal designation, the Bureau of Investigation, on March 16, 1909. As years passed, the jurisdiction of the Bureau grew, so that by the middle of the second decade of the twentieth century the workforce comprised 300 Special Agents and a like number of support personnel. Field offices were also established and agents were assigned to them, reporting back to Washington.

The entry of the United States into World War I was the impetus for still more growth in the Bureau, as violations relating to sedition, draft dodging, and espionage were put on the books. The automobile was now in full use, and with it came the crime of auto theft; the Motor Vehicle Theft Act was passed, providing the Bureau with even more jurisdiction.

The introduction of the automobile into American society also changed the nature of crime itself. Prior to the arrival of the automobile, crime was almost always a purely local matter. Crimes and the criminals who committed them were usually separated by no more than the distance a horse could travel in a day. The automobile altered that situation, resulting in many federal statutes premised on the interstate commerce clause of the Constitution; federal jurisdiction covered crimes involving the crossing of a state line.

It was also during this period that two significant, but largely forgotten, events took place: the hiring of the first female and the first African-American agents. Mrs. Alaska P. Davidson began duty as a Special Investigator on October 11, 1922. She stayed but a few years, and although two other women joined as agents shortly thereafter, they too were quickly gone. Indeed, until the death of J. Edgar Hoover in 1972, the agent population was exclusively male. So, too, with blacks. The first black Special Agent, James E. Amos, was sworn in on August 24, 1921. His career, unlike those of the women, lasted until 1955, and he worked on some of the most notorious gangster cases of that era. He was also instrumental in breaking up a major spy ring during World War II. Unfortunately, Amos was one of the few blacks in the Bureau. The agent corps was near totally white until the 1960s.

Once these sexual and racial barriers were lifted, both groups were well represented. By the end of the 1980s, both minorities and women were in executive positions within the FBI. At present, for example, there is a black female Assistant Director, while two FBI field offices are headed by black female Special Agents in Charge.

Coping with Growing Lawlessness

The name Bureau of Investigation persisted for over two decades, until July 1, 1932, when the growing entity was renamed the U.S. Bureau of Investigation. Owing to the impact of Prohibition on the U.S. psyche, on August 10, 1933, the Bureau was quickly placed under the aegis of the new Division of Investigation (BOI), a home it shared with the Bureau of Prohibition. Finally, on July 1, 1935, the FBI received its current designation as the Federal Bureau of Investigation. This was done, in part, because of prior confusion in the public's mind as to the distinction between the federal agents investigating Prohibition violations and the agents of the Bureau of Investigation.

The lawlessness of the 1920s and 1930s, with gangsters capturing the public's imagination and Prohibition wreaking havoc on society in general and law enforcement in particular, was a growth factor for the Bureau. Oftentimes federal authorities were hampered by the relative paucity of federal statutes to address serious criminal problems ranging from bootlegging and endemic corruption to the resurgence of the Ku Klux Klan. Eventually, however, the laws caught up with the times, spurred in part by notorious events such as the Lindbergh kidnapping and the antics of self-made desperados like John Dillinger, Pretty Boy Floyd, Machine Gun Kelly, and Bonnie Parker and Clyde Barrow. By the end of the 1930s, the FBI had 42 field offices, 654 Special Agents, 1,141 support employees, the beginning of the FBI Laboratory, and the FBI Identification Division as the nation's fingerprint repository. Also, in 1935, in response to growing lawlessness, the FBI started the FBI National Academy to train state and local officers. This innovation was badly needed, since at the time few states or localities offered formal training to their police forces. The Academy specifically grew out of a 1930 report by the Wickersham Commission, which called for standardization and professionalization of police training. This centralized training was enthusiastically supported by the International Association of Chiefs of Police and other law enforcement groups.

Though they had a long association with firearms, agents performed their duties without firearms—that is, when they made arrests, they made citizens arrests with the assistance of local law enforcement officers, who were armed. Agents had neither the authority to carry firearms nor the power to make arrests. But an infamous event known as the Kansas City Massacre changed that. In September 1933, several BOI agents and local law enforcement officers were escorting a prisoner in front of the Union Railway Station in Kansas City, Missouri, when they were shot down by gangsters seeking to free their friend. Special Agent Raymond Caffrey Jr. was among those killed. In May and June of 1934, in response to public outcry, Congress passed legislation giving BOI Agents the authority to make arrests and carry firearms. And once having gained this authority, the Bureau wasted no time taking advantage of it, quickly arming its agents with .38 Special revolvers, .357 Magnum revolvers, .38 Super Auto semi-automatic pistols, .45 caliber Thompson submachine guns, rifles, shotguns, the federal gas gun, and even the bulky and imposing .30-06 Colt Monitor, a civilian version of the military Browning automatic rifle. From that point forward, agents were more than prepared to tangle with even the most desperate and heavily armed criminals.

World War II, Espionage, and the Cold War

As this era was drawing to a close, another threat was developing thousands of miles away, as fascist governments began to take hold in Germany and Italy. The era before and during World War II brought the FBI into espionage and sedition investigations again as well as involved the Bureau in assisting with the protection of vital defense plants, personnel, and secrets. The FBI was highly active within the United States during this period, attempting to detect and defeat subversion and espionage activities; the Bureau even deployed agents overseas to conduct intelligence operations in support of the war effort. By the end of 1943, the FBI had approximately 4,000 agents and 9,000 support employees in a network of 54 field offices—a phenomenal rate of growth in a few years.

Indeed, this is an interesting period in FBI history, as the agents assigned to this fledgling entity—with the innocuous name of Special Investigative Services (SIS)—were in many ways the forerunner of the modern-day Central Intelligence Agency (CIA). At the same time, the Office of Strategic Services (OSS), a military operation headed by prominent New York lawyer William "Wild Bill" Donovan, was also conducting many similar operations in support of military objectives. Needless to say, there were frequent clashes between two powerful personalities of the era—Bill Donovan and J. Edgar Hoover. Eventually, in 1947, during the Truman administration, the modern CIA was formed with the passage of the National Security Act.

As a result of the legislation that created the CIA, the duties of the two agencies were divided in a somewhat simple manner. In addition to its criminal and other duties, the FBI was responsible for the detection and apprehension of spies within the United States, while the CIA was responsible for the collection of positive intelligence outside the United States. In recognition of the abuses that had taken place within Axis intelligence agencies during the just-ended war, the Act prohibited the CIA from having any domestic law enforcement authority.

The end of the war brought new challenges, as the United States entered the atomic age and needed to protect its atomic secrets, as well as conduct detailed background investigations on scientists and affiliated workers. The rise of the Soviet Union and the beginning of the Cold War brought concerns that pro-Soviet individuals would infiltrate the U.S. government in an attempt to influence policy or perform espionage operations. This time is often referred to as the "McCarthy" era, after the infamous senator from Wisconsin who used the authority of his congressional committee to interrogate and besmirch many individuals suspected of subversive activities. By the end of the Korean War, the FBI had approximately 6,200 Special Agents on duty.

Postwar Crime

As the 1950s ended and the 1960s began, the FBI was given new responsibilities in the form of federal legislation to deal with civil rights violations, gambling, and racketeering. The 1964 murder of voter-registration workers Michael Schwerner, Andrew Goodman, and James Chaney near Philadelphia, Mississippi, only intensified the public demand that civil rights violations be addressed in a forceful manner, as did the subsequent murders of Dr. Martin Luther King Jr. and Medger Evers, the Mississippi field secretary of the NAACP.

Also in the 1960s, the public, Congress, and the FBI began to appreciate the seriousness and extent of organized crime activities in the United States. Spurred first by the discovery of a huge meeting of mobsters in upstate New York by a New York State Trooper, the FBI quickly began to pay significant attention to the possibility, long discounted by the Bureau, that rumors of a national mob syndicate might be true. This was confirmed when an FBI agent persuaded La Cosa Nostra ("Mafia," in the popular parlance) member Joseph Valachi to testify publicly before a Senate Committee. Congress quickly responded with new pieces of legislation, further strengthening the Bureau's ability to address this growing menace. The two most significant pieces of legislation of the era were the Omnibus Crime Control and Safe Streets Act of 1968 and the Racketeer Influenced and Corrupt Organizations Statute of 1970, popularly known by its initials RICO.

By the end of the 1960s, the FBI had 6,703 Special Agents and 9,320 support personnel in 58 field offices and 12 Legal Attachés, the latter being FBI liaison offices attached to U.S. Embassies to coordinate investigations and share intelligence with foreign authorities. Perhaps the most dramatic moment of the 1960s was the assassination of President John F. Kennedy. Shortly after this happened, Congress made assaulting or killing the president a federal crime—which it had not been up to that point. The FBI gained jurisdiction over the investigation of such acts, it being noted that the protection of the president and other high officials remained the responsibility of the U.S. Secret Service.

The 1960s and the early 1970s also saw the rise of the counterculture revolution, loosely termed the "'60s" and aggravated by opposition to the Vietnam War. While most protest was peaceful, a fair amount was not, with an estimated 3,000 bombings and 50,000 bomb threats taking place in 1970 alone. Other groups, driven by their own particular opposition to "the establishment," also resorted to various forms of lawlessness. The fatal bombing of a math center at the University of Wisconsin, the shooting deaths of four student demonstrators at Kent State University by National Guard troops, the activities of the Weathermen and the Black Liberation Army, and numerous other acts contributed to the violence and turbulence of the times, further straining the resources of the FBI. The terrorist-led attacks on Israeli athletes, coaches, and security personnel at the Munich Olympics in 1972 were a harbinger of the modern terrorism, which brought new challenges to the FBI, and law enforcement in general, as the lines between police and military functions began to blur. Along with the social unrest came political turmoil of unprecedented magnitude, when the events commonly known as Watergate took place. Watergate deeply involved the FBI in a political corruption investigation that ultimately resulted in the resignation of President Richard M. Nixon.

By the late 1970s, the FBI had about 8,000 Special Agents and 11,000 support employees in 59 field offices and 13 Legal Attachés. Then, the 1980s brought new challenges to the American public in the form of organized criminal gangs that operated on an international basis, the rise in drug smuggling, the multi-billion dollar Savings and Loan crisis, and espionage committed by U.S. citizens against their own country. The FBI was given concurrent jurisdiction over drug matters with the Drug Enforcement Administration (DEA) to better bring the forces of both agencies to bear on the burgeoning drug problem. There were so many major spy cases brought—such as the infamous John Walker family spy ring—that the press deemed 1985 "The Year of the Spy." Also during this period, significant terrorist incidents around the world caused the FBI to make terrorism one of its priority investigative programs. In addition, this era saw the FBI begin to develop its ability to investigate matters involving computers, as these powerful new tools began to be used in criminal and intelligence activities. By 1988, the FBI had 9,663 Special Agents and 13,651 support employees serving in 58 field offices and 15 Legal Attachés.

Global and Domestic Threats

The early 1990s continued to provide both challenges and opportunities for the FBI. With the collapse of the Soviet Union, the FBI was able to re-deploy hundreds of agents formerly working counter-espionage cases to address the growing activities of violent street gangs, which had helped account for a 40 percent increase in violent crimes over a 10-year period. At the same time, the scientific possibilities of using DNA analysis in criminal investigations forever changed the nature of the investigative landscape and allowed many old cases to be reopened. The shootings and deaths of extremist elements at both Ruby Ridge, Idaho, and Waco, Texas, challenged the FBI to better deal with crisis situations.

As the twenty-first century approached, the FBI began to greatly increase its global orientation to deal with criminal, terrorist, and intelligence problems abroad. Sensing that the newly emerging free societies would need assistance establishing effective, democratic law-enforcement agencies, in 1995 the FBI opened the first International Law Enforcement Academy in Budapest, Hungary. However, the 1993 bombing of the World Trade Center in New York City and the 1995 destruction of the Murrah Federal Building in Oklahoma City quickly reminded the Bureau that there remained serious threats at home. The Bureau established the Computer Investigations and Infrastructure Threat Assessment Center (CITAC) and Computer Analysis and Response Teams to assist agents in investigations. The FBI also launched its Innocent Images Program to deal with the growing threat of child molesters who were using the Internet to advance their interests. The Bureau also began to address large-scale abuses of the nation's massive health management system and, following passage of the Economic Espionage Act of 1996, the growing theft of corporate intellectual property and personal identities.

Victims' Assistance

Over the last three decades, there has been an increase in public awareness of the rights and needs of crime victims. Accordingly, spanning most of the crime categories listed above, and also including more traditional crimes like kidnapping, bank robbery, extortion, and hijacking, is the Office of Victim Assistance (OVA). This office was created within the FBI in 2002 to ensure that the victims of crimes investigated by the FBI are aware of, and have access to, the services and notifications required by federal law and also by the 2000 Attorney General Guidelines on Victim and Witness Assistance. In general, these guidelines mandate that the FBI will staff Victim Specialist staff positions at FBI Headquarters and its 56 field offices to ensure that victims are notified of important case events and proceedings and told of available federal, state, and local resources. Beginning in 2001, the FBI began hiring 112 full-time Victim Specialists.

Prevention of Crime—A New Mission

The beginning of the new millennium was not auspicious, as both the terrorist attacks of September 11, 2001, and the arrest of long-time FBI Agent Robert Hanssen as a key Soviet spy caused the FBI to reassess its assumptions and operations. However, as the first decade of this century moves forward, the FBI is, as always, adapting and responding to the many demands made of it. It is, however, difficult to appreciate the profound influence that the events of 9/11 had on the Bureau. For one of the few times in its history, the very premise of the FBI's operations had to change. For decades, the FBI had built its reputation on solving crimes—that is, on discovering as much as it could about what had already happened. This was the stuff of classic police work: collecting evidence, interviewing witnesses and victims, apprehending criminals, and going to trial.

After 9/11, the focus shifted—for at least some of the Bureau's programs. Now the emphasis was on collection of intelligence, disruption of terrorist groups (sometimes by arrest), and prevention of terrorist attacks. The FBI had moved from the discovery of what *had* happened to the prevention of what *could* happen. Training, rules, procedures, and even Special Agent selection criteria had to change. The manner in which intelligence data were collected and handled was reorganized, as were the Bureau's protocols for sharing the data with the broader law enforcement and intelligence communities. This change process is still under way and represents the first major reorientation since the Bureau helped protect defense plants in World War II and nuclear facilities during the Cold War.

While the FBI has always been a creature of change and evolution, as noted in its history, the imperatives flowing from the events of 9/11 required a more systemic and focused approach. Accordingly, the FBI has utilized a "reengineering" philosophy to address its future. Long popular in the private sector, the reengineering concept was embraced by the General Accounting Office in 1994 as a means for governmental agencies to reduce costs and improve operational processes. Generally, this approach requires moving from the left to the right on the chart below:

Current State	High Performing Organizations
Process-Oriented	Results-Oriented
Stove-Pipe	Matrixes
Hierarchical	Flatter; More Horizontal
Inwardly Focused	Externally Focused
Micro-Managing	Employee Empowerment
Reactive Behavior	Proactive Approaches
Avoiding Technology	Leveraging Technology
Hoarding Technology	Sharing Technology
Avoiding Risk	Managing Risk
Protecting Turf	Forming Partnerships

A blueprint for this process is available, in the public record, in the form of the FBI Strategic Plan 2004–2009. It is available on the FBI website and outlines, in considerable detail considering its sensitivity, how the FBI intends to meet the mandates of the president, the attorney general, and the newly created Director of National Intelligence in the war on terror. Other FBI investigative and training priorities are also discussed.

In seeking to achieve these transformations, the Bureau is focusing on six core processes: intelligence; information management; investigative programs; human capital; strategic planning and execution; and security management. At the same time it is, as the model above suggests, looking outward. In so doing it believes there are seven drivers in the environment that will have both external and internal consequences for the FBI as it pursues its mission: global and domestic demographic changes; revolution in communications; global economic changes; rising belief in nonmaterial values abroad; revolution in technology; revolution in security technology and practice; and changing roles in state and law enforcement capabilities.

Today's FBI

Based on its analysis of the threat environment, as set forth in the Strategic Plan, the FBI now sees seven leading theaters of threat that will likely dominate its thinking and operations over the next five years. These include:

Counterterrorism

While the frequency of state-sponsored terrorism seems to be ebbing, the proliferation of privately sponsored terrorist organizations provides cause for alarm, for the latter are more mobile, less structured, and harder to detect. This concern is amplified by their ability to operate in a coordinated fashion on an ad hoc basis. Add the potential for their use of weapons of mass destruction (WMD), and the level of concern only rises. On the domestic front, the lone-wolf terrorist may pose the greatest threat. These individuals usually operate on the fringes of some ideological extremist group and have limited resources at their disposal, but they can pose a significant threat nonetheless. A prime example is the bombing of the Oklahoma City Federal Building, perpetrated by loner Timothy McVeigh, who was convicted and executed for an act that killed almost 200 civilians. Not a formal member of any group, McVeigh was a hanger-on to many extremist groups obsessed with what they perceived as the domination of the federal government over individual and states' rights.

Counterintelligence

Contrary to conventional wisdom that the espionage threat disappeared with the dissolution of the Soviet Union, foreign intelligence services remain very active, targeting military, political, technological, and economic sites. Growth in the number of countries committing intelligence resources against U.S. interests has also meant that the FBI must have far more varied language resources than at any time in the past. The wide availability of cheap, secure means of communication makes countering these intelligence threats even more of a challenge.

Cyber Technology

The growth of the cyber world presents two distinct threats. The first is the migration of traditional criminal activity to the Internet. This criminal activity could range from fraud to child pornography and identity theft. For example, the number of convictions/pretrial diversions for cyber crimes against children has risen from about 70 in 1998 to almost 700 in 2003. The second threat is the use of the Internet by terrorist and other groups as a means of communicating and planning attacks against targets throughout the world.

Public Corruption

The flow of billions of tax dollars into the fight against terrorism will probably increase the amount and frequency of public corruption, as will the concomitant restrictions on issuance of forms of identification. For example, those charged with issuing such documents will be tempted to betray their trust for monetary gain. The public corruption work done by the Bureau is seen by many as a shining example of former Director Kelley's "quality over quantity" concept, since state and local law-enforcement officials are often ill-suited and ill-equipped to investigate the very public officials to whom they report. In the federal sector, the creation of Inspectors General in many federal agencies, some with law-enforcement authority, has assisted those individuals policing the wrongdoings of their members or of the citizens and organizations with whom they deal.

Civil Rights

While the level of hate crimes has held fairly steady, increasing international tensions and factional disputes will probably produce spikes of hate crimes in response to world events. As immigration into the United States increases and foreign political disputes spill over onto U.S. shores, civil rights issues will remain prominent. Statistically, however, the most common issue in FBI civil rights investigations is allegations of police brutality. The FBI is vigorous in investigating such matters, often to the detriment of its normally close ties to state and local law-enforcement agencies.

Transnational/National Crime

Drug trafficking alone is estimated annually to cause 30,000 deaths and $110 billion in social costs throughout the world. Human trafficking, a lesser known but even more hideous crime, is estimated to be a $7 billion annual problem. Such trafficking encompasses many crimes, from prostitution to human slavery to illegal immigration. It is important to note that, in most of these transgressions, the FBI does not focus on the illegal immigrant, the captive prostitute, or the individual drug user, but on the facilitators who profit from various forms of human misery.

White-Collar Crime

Corporate fraud continues to be a concern, as evidenced by many high-profile scandals such as those involving Enron, Tyco, Global

Crossing, and other corporations. At the same time, money laundering is on the rise, aided by technology and the growth of transnational
financial institutions. The aging of the American population is also
expected to provide opportunities for increased health-care fraud. For
example, health-care fraud, now estimated to exceed $50 billion annu-
ally, represents about 4 percent of the nation's gross domestic product
(GDP). Projections are that, by 2060, this may rise to over 14 percent
of the GDP.

In its 2005 Report on Financial Crime, the FBI listed the following
priority categories and the rationale for the emphasis on each:

- Corporate fraud. Impacts jobs and hurts investors.

- Health-care fraud. Drives up the cost of medical care.

- Mortgage fraud. Often committed by industry insiders and is
  rising rapidly.

- Identity theft. Affects millions of Americans each year.

- Insurance fraud. Costs the average family $400 to $700 per year.

- Telemarketing fraud. Especially impacts the elderly and is becoming increasingly international in origin.

- Money laundering. Can impact almost any business, regardless
  of size.

The FBI Staffing Model

For many years, there was an assumption that FBI Special Agents
could do everything—at least after some on-the-job experience. In the
1980s, this belief began to change as the Bureau realized that some
professional fields were simply too complex and fast-paced for Special
Agents to stay current. Accordingly, the Bureau began to recruit some
mid- and senior-level officials from other government agencies, the
private sector, and colleges and universities.

In the wake of 9/11, the FBI again realized that it probably could not staff the many new intelligence positions strictly with Special Agents. Accordingly, it looked to civilian and military intelligence agencies for candidates for some positions. As of early 2005, the FBI was seeking applicants with extensive experience in conducting highly complex all-source intelligence research and analysis for the following positions:

Senior Intelligence Officer for East Asia
Senior Intelligence Officer for Europe
Senior Intelligence Officer for Latin America/Africa
Senior Intelligence Officer for Near East/South Asia
Senior Intelligence Officer for Russia/Eurasia
Senior Intelligence Officer for Counterterrorism
Senior Intelligence Officer for Counterintelligence
Senior Intelligence Officer for Weapons of Mass Destruction and Proliferation
Senior Intelligence Officer for Policy
Senior Intelligence Officer for Legal Issues
Senior Intelligence Officer for Cyber Assurance
Senior Intelligence Officer for Language Technologies and Research
Senior Intelligence Officer for Information Technology
Senior Intelligence Officer for Training
Senior Intelligence Officer for Global Crime
Senior Intelligence Officer for Congressional Affairs
Financial Intelligence Officer

The FBI Directors

While, as noted earlier, the current assessment of the FBI's goals and priorities is much more rigorous than at any time in the past, in many ways the FBI's development is the history of its more significant directors. The entity now known as the FBI has, throughout its years, been headed by the following leaders:

1908–1912	Chief Examiner Stanley Finch
1912–1919	Chief A. Bruce Bielaseki
1919–1921	Director William J. Flynn
1921–1924	Director William J. Burns
1924–1972	Director J. Edgar Hoover
1973–1978	Director Clarence M. Kelley
1978–1987	Director William H. Webster
1987–1993	Director William S. Sessions
1993–2001	Director Louis J. Freeh
2001–Present	Director Robert S. Mueller III

While each director brought individual strengths, weaknesses, interests, priorities, and management styles to the position, no one surpassed J. Edgar Hoover in his influence on the organization. Hoover presided over the most dramatic period of growth in the history of the FBI, brought daring new concepts to the larger field of law enforcement, cleaned up an agency mired in politics and corruption, skillfully navigated the political and bureaucratic waters of Washington, D.C., courted Congress and deftly used the power of the press, installed innovative data and management systems, ruled with an iron fist, and greatly expanded the jurisdiction and budget of the Bureau. Indeed, his very successes bred contempt, fear, scorn, envy, and concern among some people. Hoover has been the subject of numerous books and hundreds of articles, and some of these are excellent, if not always flattering, sources of information on the man and his times. As a result of Hoover's 48-year tenure, on October 18, 1976, Congress passed a law decreeing that the director of the FBI must be appointed by the president, confirmed by the Senate, and, most important, limited to one ten-year term of office.

The limitation of a ten-year term is less than coincidental. Certainly, it was meant to prevent one director—such as J. Edgar Hoover—from dominating so powerful an agency for so many decades. But the term limit is also tied to issues concerning presidential longevity. By law, a president can serve only two terms—eight years. The idea behind the ten-year term was to separate the appointment of a director from the normal turnover of Cabinet posts that occurs with changing political administrations. Of course, the president can request, and will normally receive, the resignation of a director at any time.

To many knowledgeable observers, the second most significant director in FBI history was Clarence M. Kelley. One aspect of his tenure was sure to make him prominent in the history of the FBI: he replaced Hoover, who died suddenly on May 2, 1972. Technically, there were two interim directors after Hoover: L. Patrick Gray and William Ruckelshaus, both of whom served as acting directors from May 2, 1972, until July 9, 1973, but Kelley was the first permanent replacement.

Following a person who had such a profound influence in shaping the structure and perception of the FBI, Kelley was presented with both great challenges and unparalleled opportunities—and he dealt with both admirably. A former career FBI Special Agent and Special Agent in Charge, Kelley had for many years following his retirement been the chief of police in Kansas City, Missouri. This service gave him great exposure to the operations and needs of local law enforcement and also allowed him to benefit from much progressive thinking that was going on in the law-enforcement community outside the federal system.

Perhaps Kelley's greatest accomplishment, which continues to define the role and philosophy of the FBI, was to implement a "quality over quantity" approach. Simply put, Kelley believed that the role of the FBI had changed over time, especially as state and local law-enforcement capabilities had improved. While the search for stolen cars and interstate fugitives had been a mainstay of FBI operations for many years, this was no longer the case, as many of these investigations were ably handled by state and local agencies. Kelley wanted the Bureau to get out of the "numbers game" that had dominated FBI thinking for decades, largely because the statistics of fugitives caught and stolen property recovered played well in Congress each year during budget deliberations. Kelley wanted to reposition the FBI to deal with the new, emerging, and significant criminal justice and intelligence challenges that the FBI was uniquely suited to address, and leave the more routine matters to other law-enforcement agencies.

By the time Kelley ended his service as director, the transformation was complete and never to be challenged. He further brought more balanced and scientific testing to the Career Development Program for FBI managers and executives, and he also created the Office of Program Evaluation. This new entity was to conduct a continuous cycle of reviews of FBI operations—not to look for omissions, errors, and infractions of rules, but rather to ask more profound questions like "Should we be doing this?" Because of his foresight and disregard of blind tradition, his successors inherited a new FBI.

The current Director, Robert S. Mueller III, may be viewed by history on a par with Hoover and Kelley, given the transformational changes the FBI is going through during his tenure. Mueller had been in office only a few weeks when the terrorist attacks of 9/11 occurred. Accordingly, he has had to contend with not only increased demands to counter terrorism but also with the unprecedented reorganization of the federal government that created the Department of Homeland Security. While the Bureau is not part of that department, its relationships with it have affected FBI operations and objectives in many ways.

The FBI's Employment Opportunities

For someone potentially interested in the Special Agent position, perhaps no first step is as important as gaining an understanding of what the modern FBI really does. Later, we will explore how FBI agents perform their duties and how the demands of the job affect family, friends, and, of course, oneself.

Before we begin to explore the workings of the FBI it is important to take note of two factors that have defined and shaped the FBI throughout its almost 100-year history. The first is scope. As one can readily ascertain from the history of the organization, the FBI is a changeful place.

The FBI has by far the broadest range of responsibilities of any federal investigative agency. The FBI investigates over two hundred violations of federal law, ranging from bank robbery to political corruption, from espionage to Medicaid fraud, from aircraft crashes to crime on the high seas, from organized crime to White House pre-appointment background investigations, from hate crimes to corporate fraud, and from kidnapping to narcotics trafficking. In addition, the FBI serves as the nation's fingerprint repository; handles international criminal liaison; trains foreign, state, and local police officers; maintains the National Crime Information Center, an active data base of stolen property and wanted persons; provides criminal profiling services to law-enforcement agencies; publishes the monthly *Law Enforcement Bulletin*; maintains national reference collections of firearms, paint, and other materials; conducts thousands of Freedom of Information Act searches of its files each year; and annually performs thousands of forensic laboratory examinations for federal, state, and local agencies.

In the aftermath of 9/11, the FBI substantially increased its existing commitments to both international and domestic terrorism investigations, deploying scores of Special Agents to many of the world's most dangerous regions. It is also making unprecedented efforts to upgrade its computer systems to facilitate analysis of intelligence data and is revamping its intelligence-sharing procedures with other law-enforcement and intelligence agencies. Finally, in response to the growing influence of the Internet and the increasing awareness of the value of intellectual property, the FBI is upgrading its ability to investigate computer-related crimes. Indeed, so great is this emphasis now within the Bureau that one sees references to and profiles of "Cyber Agents" in the press from time to time.

Thus, the FBI is a complex and busy organization. It is also dynamic, which is one of its great strengths in the eyes of knowledgeable observers. Over the years the FBI has literally turned on a dime to address a new threat to U.S. interests or U.S. citizens and residents. Owing to its ability to be so adaptive, Congress, members of the Executive Branch, and the American people have come to expect FBI competence and effectiveness in the face of any challenge. As the FBI's size, prominence, and capabilities grew, the Bureau increasingly has become perceived as the nation's first line of defense. Thus, the FBI became involved in cases such as the Atlanta child murders, for which Wayne Williams was convicted of the serial, ritualistic killing of African-American children; the serial arsons of African-American churches in the South; the enforcement of fugitive actions against "deadbeat dads"; the bombings of abortion clinics and gay nightspots; the Branch Davidian standoff at Waco, Texas; the fatal tampering with Tylenol that tried to obscure a domestic murder; the sniper killings that terrorized the Washington, D.C. area; and the mysterious crash of TWA flight 800 into Long Island Sound.

As a matter of pride and policy, the FBI rarely abdicates its jurisdiction over a federal violation and rarely does the Congress or Department of Justice (DOJ) transfer it to another agency. Rather, the FBI continually monitors and adjusts its use of resources, a process referred to in the Bureau as monitoring the burn rate. At the beginning of a fiscal year, the FBI will discuss with the DOJ, Congress, and the Office of Management and Budget its view of the world and its proposed strategy to address significant investigative issues in the year to come. These discussions, often contentious, result in the FBI's going into a new fiscal year with a game plan to achieve the greatest investigative and public policy impact by adjusting the Bureau's burn rate. This allows the FBI to remain active in all of its traditional roles while being responsive to new public and political requests for help. Examples of new priorities would include: defense contract fraud in the 1970s; violent street gangs in the 1980s; white supremist groups in the 1980s and 1990s; nontraditional ethnic organized crime groups in the 1980s; the Savings and Loan crisis in the 1980s and 1990s; Medicaid fraud in the 1990s; and corporate financial misdeeds and terrorism in the first decade of the 21st century. There are critics of this approach, who believe that the Bureau's jurisdiction is too broad, that it is stretched too thin, and that the continual adjustment of burn rates puts undue strain on state and local enforcement agencies. Whatever the merits of such concerns, this system of ongoing adjustments means that agents must adjust and learn new skills throughout their careers. Thus, an organized crime Special Agent in a field office may be reassigned on a temporary or permanent basis to a violent gang task force. Agents, accordingly, tend to be generalists capable of learning quickly. Some agents, on the other hand, remain in specialized lines of investigative work for the majority of their careers.

In summary, if you are considering applying for a position with the FBI, learn the current priorities of the FBI:

1. Protect the United States from terrorist attack.

2. Protect the United States from intelligence operations and espionage.

3. Protect the United States from cyber-based attacks and high-technology crimes.

4. Combat public corruption at all levels.

5. Protect the civil rights of all Americans.

6. Combat transnational and national criminal organizations and enterprises.

7. Combat major white-collar crime.

8. Combat significant violent crime.

9. Support federal, state, county, municipal, and international partners.

10. Upgrade technology to successfully perform the FBI mission.

In short, the FBI is a proud institution upon which many demands have been made in the past and will be made in the future. It is confident of its ability but also ready to admit that its confidence is no stronger than the strength of its Special Agents and support personnel. Accordingly, the Bureau can be a demanding task master, for it must address the issues it is expected to resolve. Such demands create a vibrant, ever-changing, and enriching environment in which to work.

CHAPTER 2

Staffing and Structure

The J. Edgar Hoover FBI Building is a somewhat solemn-looking square structure that sits on Pennsylvania Avenue in Washington, D.C. Eight stories high, it occupies the block between 9th and 10th Streets and is bounded by "E" Street in the rear. The facade is with somewhat odd-looking holes in a repeated pattern. As the building was nearing completion, cost overruns necessitated using poured concrete for the exterior. The holes came from the molds into which the concrete was poured.

Prior to its move into the Hoover Building in 1972, FBI Headquarters (then called by its old name, Seat of Government) was housed in the Department of Justice building directly across the street. All of the Headquarters functions resided there, and there was also a small gymnasium in the basement where defensive tactics classes were taught and a firearms range. The FBI also used another older building, the Old Post Office Building, several blocks away for classrooms. New agents were bused to Quantico several times for firearms training and so they stayed in a modest, two-story red brick building on the nearby Marine Corps base.

It was planned that the new Hoover Building would be open to the public, at least on the ground level. There are wide ground-level entrances and an interior cobblestone courtyard. The sides of the building feature broad, sweeping steps up to the second level, and a promenade runs along the second floor. The eighth floor houses the cafeteria, a credit union, the memorabilia and clothing store run by the FBI Recreation Association, and administrative offices. The building is home to the office of the director and other senior officials, and this section is known throughout the FBI as Mahogany Row. The remainder of the building is occupied by parts of the Records Management Division and a small part of the Criminal Justice Information Services Division, formerly known as the Identification Division. "Ident," as the division is called in the FBI, was the custodian of the FBI's millions of fingerprint cards. Elsewhere in the building are offices for the various Headquarters divisions and also the Strategic Intelligence Operations Center (SIOC), a high-tech command center used by the director and the attorney general in times of emergency or to direct major cases.

The SIOC is a wonder, in and of itself. Originally created in 1989, it was upgraded in 1998 and is now capable of handling two simultaneous crisis events at the same time. It has almost 40,000 square feet of space and includes briefing theaters, a watch floor, a control room, and information support facilities. It can seat 430 people and has 1,100 telephone lines that total almost 35 miles in length, 60 miles of fiber optic cable, 235 computer terminals, and eight large video display screens.

Soon after the Hoover Building was opened, the plans for unlimited public access to the street level were scrapped for security reasons. After 9/11, still more security measures were implemented, with the result that most of the entrances have gates over them. Access by employees and approved visitors is tightly controlled, and the facility is guarded by FBI Police, who are sworn, non-Agent, law-enforcement officers.

For decades, the building was the scene of the world-famous FBI tour, and millions of visitors and tourists from around the world have taken it. Featuring displays of law-enforcement technology old and new, the tour was designed to allow visitors to observe FBI Special Agents and technicians conduct forensic examinations of evidence through glass walls built into the back of the Laboratory Division. The tour also took visitors past the FBI's massive reference collection of firearms from around the world. For many, the highlight of the tour was a shooting demonstration put on by a Special Agent firearms instructor. Unfortunately, since 9/11, the FBI closed the tour until more effective security measures and design changes can be implemented for the protection of visitors and FBI employees alike.

Major FBI Divisions and Positions

Thousands of people work in the Hoover Building; it represents the heart, soul, and brain of today's FBI. From the director to the most junior support employee, this is where the FBI's worldwide operations are run. The operations are executed in the field, but they are directed from this location. The building never shuts down, as some functions are manned 24 hours a day, 365 days a year.

To accomplish its complex mission and direct its far-flung and wide-ranging activities, the FBI requires numerous personnel and substantial coordination. Accordingly, the director has a large staff that supports him in this process. While the director has ultimate authority over the operations delegated to him by the attorney general, on paper at least he has but one body that directly reports to him: the Special Agents In Charge (SAC) Advisory Committee. This is a group of SACs selected by their peers to provide the director with field input on matters of policy and practice. The group cannot overrule the director, but it does keep him informed of field concerns and interests. Like many large organizations, there is often contention between how Headquarters executives and field executives see the world. The Advisory Committee is an attempt to bridge that gap.

Much of the support the director receives flows through the office

of his principal deputy, the deputy director. This person has nine entities reporting to him:

- *Chief of Staff.* A fairly new position, the incumbent of this position acts as an assistant to the deputy director. The function of
  a chief of staff is not only to act as a gatekeeper but also to
  ensure that policy amendments reaching the deputy director are
  "fully staffed." That is, that all necessary coordination and input
  have been reflected in policy documents before they are presented to the deputy director for consideration.

- *Inspection Division.* The personnel assigned to this office conduct periodic operational and compliance inspections of all FBI
  field offices, Legal Attachés, Resident Agencies, and Headquarters Divisions. The division has a small permanent staff, but is
  augmented by agents detailed to it for one- or two-year periods,
  as exposure to the work of the division is deemed crucial to
  future career development. Every operating entity within the FBI
  is subject to an inspection on roughly a biannual basis. The division's inspection findings are viewed with utmost concern by
  FBI executives, as they reflect the operational readiness of the
  FBI to fulfill its many disparate missions.

- *Office of Public Affairs.* The FBI is the source of many news
  stories, research requests, and fictionalized depictions. It is difficult to pick up any major U.S. newspaper for more than two
  or three consecutive days and not see some story about or reference to the FBI. Each of these stories breeds inquiries and com-
  ments. The role of this office is to be the bridge between the FBI
  and the public. Any script writer, author, or producer can con-
  sult with the FBI regarding closed cases, history, and to some
  degree, current operations and capabilities. There is, however,
  no requirement that they do so. Further, the FBI does not edit
  or approve scripts or stories.

- *Congressional Affairs Office.* Because of its prominence and
  wide range of responsibilities, the FBI is subject to oversight by

a number of congressional committees. These include the House and Senate Judiciary Committees, the House and Senate Intelligence Committees, the House and Senate Appropriations Committees, the House Government Reform Committee, and the Senate Government Affairs Committee. This office coordinates those relationships and also answers inquiries by individual members of Congress on behalf of their constituents.

- *Office of the Ombudsman.* This office is the channel by which any FBI employee can direct concerns or complaints about FBI operations or personnel. Sometimes, the ombudsman will recommend changes to FBI policies if they are not functioning as intended or are having unintended impacts on certain employees.

- *Office of General Counsel.* Again, given the wide range and sensitive nature of many FBI operations, this office provides both the director and operating FBI divisions with legal analysis and support. The office contains a Litigation Branch, an Administrative and Technology Law Branch, a Legal Advice and Training Branch, and a National Security Law Branch.

- *Chief Information Officer.* Noting that the FBI is in many ways a vast collector and analyzer of information, this person advises the director on information and technology policy.

- *Office of Equal Employment Opportunity.* Like all federal agencies, the FBI must strive to ensure that all employees are treated in a fair and consistent manner. The office is also active in promoting the recruitment of minority candidates to the FBI.

- *Office of Professional Responsibility* (OPR). This office is charged with investigating any allegation of violation of law or any serious breach of FBI policy by FBI personnel. The office has the authority to investigate any FBI employee suspected of wrongdoing, up to and including the director. Indeed, one director was dismissed from his position by the president on the basis of an OPR inquiry.

The Second Tier

Were there not enough already on his plate, the deputy director also has five executive assistant directors (EAD) reporting up through him. The EAD position is relatively new in the FBI, having been created in the 1970s by then-director William H. Webster. It was intended to bring greater coordination among FBI Headquarters divisions with related areas of responsibility. The five EADs are:

- *EAD—Intelligence.* This is the only EAD who has a single entity reporting to him, the Office of Intelligence. Its responsibility is to ensure that the investigative resources of the FBI are properly aligned to counter emerging and evolving national security and criminal threats. It is also charged with providing information and analysis to other agencies involved in homeland security, law enforcement, and national security. The office also seeks to ensure that the FBI has consistent intelligence policies, has adequate intelligence resources, and has aligned operations and capabilities to address emerging threats.

- *EAD—Counterterrorism/Counterintelligence.* This EAD has two divisions reporting to him: the Counterterrorism Division and the Counterintelligence Division. The Counterterrorism Division strives to learn of and defeat terrorist plots against the United States, usually by nongovernmental groups and entities. The Counterintelligence Division strives to learn of and defeat, often through criminal prosecution, the efforts of other nations to learn U.S. secrets. The responsibilities of this division were expanded significantly with the passage of the Economic Espionage Act of 1996, which made it illegal for any person or nation to attempt to steal U.S. trade secrets. Thus, the protections long afforded state and military secrets were extended to the private sector.

- *EAD—Criminal Investigations.* This individual has two divisions reporting to him: the Cyber Division and the Criminal

Investigative Division. The Cyber Division is charged with learning of and investigating threats to persons and entities through use of cyber devices. The division also protects the nation's cyber infrastructure through a partnership relationship with the National Infrastructure Protection Center. It fosters public–private partnerships to advance the capabilities of all U.S. law-enforcement agencies to deal with cyber threats. The Criminal Investigative Division is where the bulk of the FBI's traditional jurisdiction resides, being charged with investigating everything from bank robberies to corporate misdeeds to mob bosses. All told, the division is responsible for the investigation of well over 100 violations of federal criminal law.

- **EAD—Law Enforcement Services.** This individual has seven entities reporting to him and functions as the FBI's primary interface with the U.S. and foreign law-enforcement communities:

1. Office of Law Enforcement Coordination. This entity addresses issues of information sharing and joint responsibilities with other law-enforcement agencies.

2. Office of International Operations. This is the office to which the FBI's wide network of Legal Attachés report.

3. Critical Incident Response Group. This is the group that develops policy and coordinates resources in the event of major incidents. These could include the abduction of children, crisis management, hostage situations, and more. Founded in 1994, it seeks to ensure that appropriate law-enforcement resources are brought to bear on major incidents quickly. The group is also responsible for training FBI undercover agents.

4. Training Division. This is name for the FBI Academy at Quantico, Virginia, where new FBI agents, veteran agents, and police officers from around the United States and the world receive training. The Training Division also coordinates the substantial training provided in field offices to state and local law-enforcement officers.

5. Laboratory Division. This division conducts scientific fo-

rensic investigations for the FBI as well as state, local, and some foreign law-enforcement agencies. It also provides support in the areas of crime scene searches, DNA testing, aircraft and other disaster incidents, and court testimony.

6. Criminal Justice Information Services Division. This is the old Identification Division and, as such, is the keeper of the nation's fingerprint archives. In the past, it was the repository for 32 million paper fingerprint cards (which, if stacked, would be 13 times as high as the Empire State Building). In the 1980s, largely through the sponsorship of Senator Robert Byrd, of West Virginia, the division was moved to a new $185 million facility in West Virginia. Since that time, over $1 billion in additional funding has been provided to automate the formerly labor-intensive examination process. It is now highly automated and over 98 percent of the time can determine in two hours if a suspect has an outstanding warrant or criminal history.

In addition to managing the Fingerprint Identification Program, the division is also responsible for the National Crime Information Center (NCIC), a decades-old program. Using NCIC, law-enforcement authorities throughout the United States can check if persons in their custody are wanted for other crimes or if recovered vehicles or property were reported stolen. The division also runs the Uniform Crime Reporting (UCR) program, which is the official annual report of crime rates in the United States, compiled from reporting agencies around the country, and the Integrated Automated Fingerprint Identification System, which is a computer-based system that can store, analyze, and retrieve millions of fingerprints in a short period of time.

The UCR program, which began in 1929, deserves special mention for it is little known outside of law enforcement, public policy, research, and academic circles. Most people in the United States are familiar with it from newspaper headlines announcing that crime in a certain city or area was up or down from the previous year. The program does, however, have many other far-reaching uses. The UCR data, which is contributed by 17,000 agencies covering 93 percent of the U.S. population, tracks major categories of crime, such as homicide, forcible rape, robbery, aggravated assault, burglary, larceny, theft, motor vehicle theft, and arson. Twenty-two lesser violations of law are also tracked, as are hate crimes. The UCR data is used by politicians, policymakers, academics, planners, and budget officials across the country who must deal with criminal justice programs and policies. The data, which are available to the public, are also used by industries such as insurance companies to measure policy risk.

7. Investigative Technologies Division. This is a new division, devoted to the development and utilization of advanced technologies in the conduct of investigations. It includes many technological forms—computers, audio, and video.

- *EAD—Administration.* This position has six divisions reporting to it and functions as the infrastructure keeper of the FBI:

1. Office of Strategic Planning. Started under Director William H. Webster as the Long Range Planning Staff, this entity is charged with researching future responsibilities that may be placed on the FBI and anticipating future resource requirements. The office was created to attempt to counter a tendency in the FBI and most public and private organizations—the intense focus on present concerns to the detriment of planning for future responsibilities.

2. Security Division. This entity is charged with ensuring the protection of FBI personnel and facilities and also for the protection of FBI-sensitive information.

3. Finance Division. The FBI is a multi-billion dollar operation and must formulate and execute a budget each year. It must also report its financial affairs to the Department of Justice, the

Office of Management and Budget, and various congressional committees. The assistant director of this division is the FBI's chief financial officer and also the chair of the Contract Review Board. The FBI must also comply with voluminous federal regulations on the awarding of contracts and the purchase of goods and services; the division also sets yearly budgets for divisions and field offices for any number of goods and services ranging from gasoline and ammunition, to informant payments, vehicles, and rental space.

4. Records Management Division. The FBI collects and generates tremendous amounts of information. This division is charged with the maintenance, retrieval, security, and dissemination of that information. The division is also responsible for managing the thousands of Freedom of Information Act requests the FBI receives each year from citizens, academics, journalists, researchers, and others.

5. Administrative Services Division. This division is the FBI's back office, charged with recruiting, testing, background investigations, performance management, staffing, development and implementation of personnel policies, transfers, medical policy, pay and benefits, insurance, retirement, discipline, space and fleet management, physical security, printing and supply management, and policy direction of the FBI's nonagent employees.

6. Information Resources Division. This is the Management Information Systems (MIS) department of the FBI, charged with keeping its computer infrastructure up and running.

Joint Operations

In addition to its Headquarters divisions and offices, the FBI also participates in joint enterprises with other agencies. One of these, the Terrorist Screening Center, was mandated by Homeland Security Directive 6, signed on September 16, 2003, and it became operational on December 1, 2003. The center is charged with ensuring that federal, state, and local law-enforcement personnel and transportation screeners have the information to deal with a known or suspected terrorist who is encountered in the United States, at the borders, or at a U.S. Embassy. Personnel from the FBI, Homeland Security, Department of State, and the Department of the Treasury staff the center.

Likewise, the FBI participates in the activities of the Financial Analysis Center (FinCEN), a multi-agency entity created in 1990 and devoted to combating money laundering. Initially established to address the movement of illegal funds in narcotics, organized crime, and tax evasion, the work of the center grew to monitor the movement of funds in conjunction with terrorism operations. The center has about 200 employees, many of whom are intelligence professionals, financial industry specialists, and technology specialists. Among the 20 other law-enforcement and regulatory agencies participating in the center's operations are the Internal Revenue Service, the Drug Enforcement Administration, and the U.S. Marshals Service.

The FBI also participates in the deliberations of the Financial Action Task Force (FATF), an inter-agency group chaired by the U.S. Department of State. The group is charged with the development of all anti-money laundering policy within the United States and also with seeking international cooperation in the fight against money laundering.

In response to the growing terrorist threat around the world, the FBI participates in the Terrorist Explosives Device Analytical Center (TEDAC), an FBI-led initiative created in December 2003. The objective of the center is to collect from worldwide sources complete forensic and technical analysis of every explosive device used by terrorists and then disseminate this information to the law-enforcement, intelligence, and military communities. The center is staffed with electronics specialists, explosives experts, terrorism agents and analysts, and engineers from a variety of agencies. In addition to the FBI, the Bureau of

Alcohol, Tobacco, Firearms and Explosives, the Federal Air Marshal Service, members of the U.S. Intelligence Community, and persons from the Department of Defense participate.

Special Programs and Partnerships

The FBI has run the Special Event Management Program ever since its creation in 1978. The first operational use of that program was for the Pan American Games in San Juan, Puerto Rico. FBI presence at events such as national political conventions, the Olympics, the Super Bowl, and other high-profile gatherings is meant to provide increased security and better coordination with other law-enforcement agencies. It is not meant to stifle lawful protests, but rather concentrates on possible violations of federal law and the suppression of violence. Unlawful behavior at such venues is more common than often thought. For example, at the Free Trade of the Americas meetings in November 2003, local police were attacked with marbles and bolts fired from sling shots and wrist rockets, rocks, sticks with razors and nails embedded in them, and bleach and urine.

For many years, but especially in the last two decades, the FBI has also forged new and innovative alliances with public and private-sector groups. A prime example is INFRA GARD, a program started in the Cleveland field office in 1996. It has since spread to all FBI field offices. INFRA GARD is a program to share information and analysis regarding the protection of America's critical national infrastructure. The program involves businesses, academic institutions, state and local entities, and other groups. Each chapter has a Special Agent coordinator from the local FBI field office. The goals and objectives of the program are to increase the level of information sharing and reporting of cyber incidents; provide members threat advisory information; increase liaison with and among state, local, and federal agencies; and provide members a forum for education and training on cyber threats. In 2005, there were over 15,000 members in the INFRA GARD program.

The FBI also has a partnership with the National White Collar Crime Center to operate the Internet Crime Complaint Center (IC3), through which citizens can report crimes committed against them through the use of the Internet. Originally founded as the Internet Fraud Complaint Center, the entity has grown to encompass a range of misdeeds, to include intellectual property rights matters, computer intrusions, economic espionage, on-line extortion, international money laundering, and other Internet-facilitated crimes. IC3 refers these matters for investigation and also works with other agencies, the private sector, and the public to reduce the incidence of such crimes.

Finally, the FBI has a memorandum of understanding with the Police Futurists International. This group uses a combination of mathematical models, study of the past, cross-disciplinary analysis of events and problems, expert evaluation, and systems-analytical problem analysis to predict future challenges to law enforcement. The group specializes in matters judged to be mid-level (five to ten years out) to distant (50 or more years out). By participating in such an endeavor, the FBI seeks not only to improve its understanding of future challenges but also to better prepare for meeting the needs of the law-enforcement entities it supports thorough its Law Enforcement Services function.

The Further Chain of Command

FBI divisions are headed by an assistant director in charge, who is assisted by an inspector/deputy assistant director and one or more section chiefs and unit chiefs. Offices such as the Congressional Affairs Office are typically headed by an inspector/deputy assistant director. An FBI division may have as few as a hundred or so employees, while others may have well over a thousand. Offices typically have about 20 to 50 employees.

In performing their duties, these various Headquarters' divisions and offices deal with each other, with the field offices, with the Department of Justice, with other governmental entities, and with the public. The manner in which they deal with the field is perhaps the most complex. It is best to view this relationship from the perspective of the field executive to gain a sense of its intricacy.

There are 56 FBI field offices and about 400 resident agencies, or suboffices. The largest of these offices is headed by an assistant director in charge, assisted by one or more Special Agents in Charge (SAC, always pronounced by its individual letters, *S-A-C*) and Assistant Special Agents in Charge (ASAC, always pronounced as one word, *a-sack*). Most FBI field offices, however, have only an SAC and one or more ASACs. Within each field office there are a number of squads, each headed by a Supervisory Special Agent (SSA). These squads will be semi-specialized and may work organized crime, white-collar crime, terrorism, violent crime, or intelligence matters. One of the changes to the FBI following the events of 9/11 was the creation of an intelligence squad in each field office, known as a Field Intelligence Group.

If the Bureau were to come out with a new policy on investigating bank robberies, it would come from the Criminal Investigative Division. If an SAC had concerns or questions about the policy change, they would deal with that division. Later in the day, if the SAC wanted approval to modify the manner in which records were kept in the field office, they would deal with the Records Management Division. If an agent were injured in an automobile accident and had to be put on limited duty, the individual would deal with the Administrative Services Division. Thus, the relationship between the field and headquarters is issue-driven. This puts a premium on coordination at the Headquarters level, so that conflicting advice and direction are not provided to the field. Generally, all FBI policies apply evenly to all field offices, absent issues of size or unusual conditions.

Policy changes in the FBI are never made in a vacuum nor are they spur-of-the-moment decisions. Each is carefully researched and voluminous documentation will be created to justify each change. Because of the complexity of FBI scope and operations, coordination with other divisions is the norm. Much time at FBI Headquarters is spent researching, writing, and debating policy changes, so good writing and analytical skills are a must for those in most Headquarters' positions. So, too, is the ability to function well in meetings, as many Headquarters' hours are devoted to intra- and inter-divisional meetings.

Staffing of Agents and Nonagents

FBI Headquarters also has a profound impact on FBI field operations: it sets staffing levels. Once a year the agent and nonagent personnel staffing of each field office are reviewed and adjustments are made to reflect population growth; changes in criminal, terrorist, or intelligence activity in the area; movement of significant or sensitive industries into the area; and other factors. These changes may take place fairly quickly or over a longer period of time, depending on whether the office is gaining or losing personnel. For offices that have gained staffing, personnel may be transferred into them. Nonagent jobs are posted throughout the FBI and qualified personnel can apply for them. Those selected will be given full-cost government-paid transfers. Offices gaining agent increases will normally be augmented by transfers of new agents coming out of Quantico. Offices losing staff will do so more slowly, since normal FBI policy is to let these reductions take place over time through attrition.

Additionally, there is the issue of support staff. Well over half of the people in the FBI are nonagent support employees, and without them the FBI would not run. The FBI's philosophy on nonagent personnel has changed markedly over the years and the Bureau is stronger because of it.

For decades the conventional wisdom in the FBI was that agents could do everything. They held laboratory, financial, information technology, and other positions, and for many years this system worked well. Nonagent personnel were important, but they tended to hold lower-level positions in word processing, file management, or fingerprint identification. However, beginning in the early 1970s, the

FBI realized that while agents may have had appropriate backgrounds before coming into the Bureau or gained substantial knowledge performing duties on the job, this was not the best answer for meeting the FBI's needs. Technology was simply moving too quickly for someone who had spent a significant amount of his career performing investigative duties to be current. Plus, the demands of the Career Development Program tended to move agents around, limiting their ability to develop in-depth expertise.

Accordingly, use of nonagent personnel was broadened, with more and more responsibilities shifted to their ranks. Today there are nonagents at every level of the FBI, to include assistant directors. Some have come up through the ranks while others were lateral entries from the private sector or other government agencies. Like agents, they all hold Top Secret clearances and have had full field background investigations. They serve as budget officers, property management executives, information technology specialists, translators, forensic scientists, engineers, instructors, librarians, administrators, attorneys, medical specialists, human resources managers, financial analysts, intelligence analysts, vehicle fleet administrators, contract administrators, plumbers, carpenters, pilots, armorers, and security personnel. For many of these nonagents, the FBI offers as important and fulfilling a career as those of Special Agent, and the service records of these individuals are often remarkable.

Pay and Benefits

Within the federal civil service, the FBI is what is known as an excepted service within the executive branch of government, which means that the Bureau is not bound by all of the regulations and procedures that pertain to personnel actions in other governmental agencies. This longstanding status was provided the FBI in recognition of the unusual nature of many of its operational requirements. Other agencies, such as the Central Intelligence Agency, are also considered to be excepted services. That being said, the FBI operates its personnel functions in a manner similar to most other agencies. In this chapter, we examine the various categories of pay and the benefits that pertain to FBI agents as civil service employees.

Salary Grades and Promotions

FBI Special Agents are paid on a General Service (GS) scale that runs from GS-1 through GS-15. In the past, the scale ran to GS-18, but the levels GS-16 through GS-18 were replaced with the introduction of the Senior Executive Service (SES) concept into the federal government in the late 1980s. SES grades run from SES-1 through the highest grade, SES-6. Within each grade on the GS scale there are 10 sublevels, or "steps." Thus, a newly appointed Special Agent will, absent prior federal civilian service, start as a GS-10, or step 1. Steps are also referred to as within-grade increases, or "Ramspecks," after the name of the legislator who sponsored the bill that made them part of the civil service system.

The function of these steps is to reward longevity within a given GS grade. For example, an individual in a GS-10, step 1 position ($49,818 at this time), such as a new agent, would be promoted to GS-10, step 2 ($51,479) after one year's satisfactory service. This process continues as long as the individual is in that grade, although the intervals between promotions increase from one year to three years at the higher end of the GS-10 step scale. Thus, an individual might have to serve three years to go from GS-10, step 8, to GS-10, step 9.

This situation is somewhat academic for most new agents, assuming they are performing in a satisfactory manner. After two years' satisfactory service as a GS-10, they are promoted to GS-11, step 1 (currently $54,735). While new agents are serving in that grade, the step progressions continue. After two years' satisfactory service as a GS-11, they are promoted to GS-12, step 1 ($65,602), and following three years' satisfactory service as a GS-12, they are promoted to GS-13, step 1 ($78,012). In each grade, the step progressions continue. Assuming they do not seek administrative advancement and move into management ranks, which begin at GS-14, they end their careers as GS-13s, probably in the 10th step of that grade (currently $101,413). Under current FBI policy, a new agent coming out of Quantico and performing satisfactorily will reach GS-13, step 1, after seven years' service.

One of the features of the within-grade system is that someone cannot, by law, lose money when getting a promotion. Per federal law, an employee who is promoted to a higher grade must be put into a step within that new grade that is equal to or exceeds his current salary. However, this rarely applies to "street" agents, since they are rarely in a grade long enough to be in a high enough step to exceed step 1 of the next higher grade. For example, an agent would have to be in GS-11, step 7, to exceed the starting salary in GS-12, step 1. Where this situation might occur is with somewhat senior GS-13 agents who accept administrative advancement by going into the Career Development Program (CDP). Were they a GS-13, step 7 ($93,612), they would exceed GS-14, step 1 ($92,186). Accordingly, upon being promoted, they would be placed into GS-14, step 2 ($95,259).

Like all federal employees, FBI agents receive annual adjustments to their pay based on calculations made by the U.S. Department of Labor. These are not exactly inflationary adjustments and are often subject to the politics of the day in Washington. Unfortunately, often the increases are offset by increases in health-care premiums.

Almost all personnel in FBI field offices are eligible for locality pay adjustments, also known as cost of living adjustments (COLAs). These adjustments are set by the federal government and are in recognition of the fact that, in some geographic areas, the federal salaries are simply not competitive with those in the private sector. COLAs can range as high as 25 percent of base pay. Thus, new agents assigned to a high-cost area such as New York City earn approximately $75,000, with their COLA adjustment and Availability Pay (AVP; discussed below).

Overtime Pay

Upon graduating from New Agents Training and being assigned to a field office, agents become eligible for availability pay (AVP), the equivalent of overtime pay. AVP is one of the longest standing and to some, most controversial, personnel practices within the FBI. Few within the Bureau complain about it, but various other government agencies, congressional committees, and some newspapers have attacked it from time to time. That it has survived for so many decades speaks to its imminent practicality and utility.

FBI agents do not earn overtime, even though on occasion they may be working 10-, 12-, or 16-hour days. For decades, police departments have wrestled with the problem of overtime for detectives and investigators. Simply put, crimes, especially major crimes, do not often happen at convenient times. There is also an old mantra in law enforcement that says, with much justification, that crimes are easiest to solve when they are fresh. Witnesses are handy, memories are sharper, evidence as abundant as it will ever be, perpetrators are still relatively close by, alibis have not had time to be fully developed, vehicles and weapons have not been disposed of, and loot has not been hidden or laundered. There is a lot of logic for throwing substantial resources at a significant crime as soon as it happens.

But in light of all this logic, consider the plight of the typical, budget-constrained police department: The crime occurs at 1:30 P.M. Uniformed officers, detectives, and FBI agents respond. By 3:00 P.M. some promising leads are beginning to develop. Joint strategy sessions are held. Leads are assigned. Surveillances commence. Then, 4:00 P.M. hits. The detectives are on day tour and go off duty, or must request permission to work overtime from their superiors. Sometimes, the temptation is to replace the day-tour detectives with those coming on duty for the 4–12 shift, but if this is done, all the institutional knowledge of the crime and the perpetrators go home with the day-tour detectives. Certainly, there can be a hand-off of notes and information, but the information is hardly ever complete.

This is the dilemma faced every day by most major police departments in the United States. It is also a dilemma that came to the attention of J. Edgar Hoover during his long tenure as director. His response was to get authority to implement the AVP system (then known as voluntary overtime, or VOT, and later as administratively uncontrollable overtime, or AUO). The system was a form of "automatic" overtime, in which all FBI agents would receive 25 percent of their base salary automatically in exchange for being available 24 hours a day, if needed. Over the years the Bureau has constructed several fairly complicated systems to collect data on the number of hours agents work on given days and over given periods, and an agent who falls below a rolling average for a period may lose part or all of his AVP pay. But by and large, this does not happen. The AVP system gives FBI field managers great flexibility in dealing with crimes and other activities. Likewise, the agents like the predictability of the AVP system, unlike overtime systems that can vary widely from month to month.

Almost all agents believe the AVP system is fair to both the agents and the Bureau, even though they probably wind up working more overtime than they are paid for during the course of a year. AVP pay is also included in the annuity calculation made when an agent is eligible to retire.

Vacation Time

Annual leave (AL) is the equivalent of vacation days in the private sector. Full-time employees in the FBI earn AL at a rate determined by their years of federal government service. Thus, someone entering the FBI as a former federal employee, even one who did not hold a law-enforcement position, will be credited with this service time for AL purposes. FBI agents earn AL at the rate of 13 days a year for their first three years of service. After three years and up to 15 years of service, they earn just under four weeks' AL a year. After 15 years of service they earn just over five weeks' AL a year.

AL can be used for any purpose, although it must be taken with the permission of the agent's supervisor. On rare occasions, an AL request may be denied owing to the demands of the office, but every effort is made to accommodate any reasonable AL request. AL that is not used can normally be carried forward to the next year, with a cap of one year's entitlement. Thus, an agent with fewer than three years' service could carry up to 13 days AL from one year to the next. At least the amount of AL carried forward must be used in the succeeding calendar year or it will be forfeited. In some instances it may be possible for one agent to transfer a portion of his accumulated AL to another agent who may be experiencing personal or family problems that require extended time off.

Sick Leave, Holidays, Family and Medical Leaves

Sick leave (SL) is earned at the rate of four hours per two-week period, or 13 days a year. SL can be used for any legitimate medical purpose and can be carried forward, without limitation, from year to year. In certain circumstances, SL can be used for other purposes as well; these are discussed below. AL can be combined with SL if an employee is out for a period of time that exceeds his SL hours accumulated. SL, however, cannot be combined with AL to extend time off for a vacation or other nonmedical purpose.

As federal employees, FBI agents are granted 10 paid federal holidays each year. These include New Year's Day, Martin Luther King's Birthday, President's Day, Memorial Day, Independence Day, Labor Day, Columbus Day, Veterans Day, Thanksgiving, and Christmas. It is possible to combine AL with these holidays to permit extended time off.

Family and medical leave is also available. An agent may be granted up to 12 weeks of unpaid leave in any 12-month period for the birth of, or care for, a child; the placement of a child with the employee for adoption or foster care; the care of a spouse, son, daughter, or parent if that person has a serious medical condition; or a serious health condition of the agent himself, if this condition renders him unable to perform one or more of the essential elements of his position. To be eligible for these benefits the agent must have completed at least one year of service.

Maternity leave is granted as a leave of absence when an agent intends to return to her position. Generally, this period does not exceed six months. While the agent is physically incapacitated, she is charged SL. When she is physically released by her doctor, she is charged with AL or a combination of AL and leave without pay (LWOP).

Paternity leave may be granted to a male agent who must care for a newborn or other child when the mother is incapacitated for maternity reasons. The agent may take up to five days' SL for this purpose or, under some conditions, eight days' SL.

Family-friendly leave is permitted to care for a family member or to arrange for or attend the funeral of a close relative. Up to 40 hours' (eight days) SL may be used for this purpose. In certain circumstances, an additional 64 hours' SL may also be utilized. Additional forms of leave may also be available, such as adoption leave; leave for bone marrow and organ donations; military leave; leave for voting; court leave; and jury-witness leave. Under certain limited circumstances it is possible for an employee to resign from the FBI to enter the full-time military service of the United States and be reinstated, without loss of pay, benefits, or position, when that period of military service ends.

Funeral leave is permitted in some circumstances to attend a funeral for a law-enforcement, line-of-duty death. Travel expenses may also be reimbursed.

Retirement Benefits

All persons entering the federal civil service after 1983 are automatically part of the Federal Employees Retirement System (FERS). FERS is a three-part retirement plan that combines a noncontributory basic annuity benefit, the Thrift Savings Plan, and Social Security. Once an employee has worked for the federal government for five years, he is eligible for an annuity, which is a monthly benefit paid for life upon reaching a qualifying age. Also, at achieving five years of civilian service, the individual can gain credit for any prior military service, although he may be required to pay a deposit into the retirement system to gain maximum credit for these years.

Newly hired FBI agents can retire when they reach age 50 and also have 20 years of federal civilian law-enforcement experience or when they have 25 years of federal civilian law-enforcement experience, regardless of age. Agents must retire by no later than the end of the month in which they reach age 57, assuming they have completed at least 20 years of federal civilian law-enforcement duty. The director of the FBI has the authority to waive this requirement when it is in the best interests of the FBI. Such waivers are relatively rare.

When agents retire they are eligible for an annuity that is based on a formula that considers their length of service and the highest salaries they have earned during their careers. This annuity is paid monthly and is adjusted to some degree for inflation. They are also eligible for Social Security at age 62 if they were hired after 1983. Disability Social Security benefits are conditionally available at any age.

The Thrift Savings Plan (TSP) is a retirement and investment vehicle that operates in many ways like a 401K plan in the private sector. Monies put into the TSP are not taxable, although future payments from the TSP will be taxed as income. All persons covered by FERS are eligible to contribute up to 10 percent of their salaries to the TSP, although some Internal Revenue Service deposit limitations may apply. The FBI automatically contributes an amount equal to 1 percent of the agent's salary, even if the individual chooses to contribute nothing to the TSP. In addition, the FBI matches the agent's contributions dollar for dollar for the first 3 percent contributed to the plan and then 50 cents on the dollar for the next 2 percent contributed.

All contributions to the TSP earn interest and can be allocated by the agent to one or more of three investment vehicles: one based on government securities, one based on stocks, and one based on bonds. Should an employee choose to leave the FBI prior to becoming eligible for retirement, the individual may ask for a refund of the money deposited in the TSP, although some early distribution regulations may apply. The alternative is to leave the money in the account and allow it to continue to earn interest.

Relocation Benefits

Since transfers are a way of life in the FBI, the Bureau pays for a five-day house-hunting trip for a new agent coming out of training and his or her spouse. This trip is not charged against AL. Agents already assigned to field offices or new agents who were prior federal employees are eligible for 10-day house-hunting trips. The Bureau will also pay to move household goods. The agent is also eligible to try to sell his or her residence for the best price possible. If, after a period of several months, the individual has been unable to sell the house, he or she can use a Bureau program in which a private company under contract to the government has the house professionally appraised and then offers to buy it from the agent at that price. There is no requirement that an agent use this service, but it does provide some protection if someone is located in a slow housing market.

While not technically a benefit, the FBI is also cognizant of the needs of a special group of employees: married agent couples (MACs). Throughout the first five decades of its history, when the Special Agent force was all male (with a few notable exceptions early on), marriages between male agents and female support employees were somewhat common. They still are, but with the arrival of female agents in 1972, the FBI was faced with a new challenge.

In the past, if a male agent was transferred or promoted, it was a fairly simple task to transfer the support employee spouse with the agent to a new FBI position in another office or at FBI Headquarters. Now, with the advent of MACs, the transfer situation became somewhat more complicated. This was particularly true if one spouse was in the Career Development Program and the other was not. The FBI's Special Agent Transfer Unit (SATU) has been both persistent and creative in dealing with the transfer challenges created by MACs. Generally, an acceptable transfer strategy can be developed to maintain the viability of the MAC's lifestyle, while still meeting the operational needs of the FBI. This is not to suggest that all such issues are perfect in their resolution, but much progress and accommodation has been achieved.

Health Care and Child Care

Agents stationed at FBI Headquarters or in some of the larger field offices can avail themselves of the services of the Health Care Program

Unit (HCPU). Agents in smaller offices can also be served by the unit but the contact is less direct. This unit is staffed with medical professionals and specialists and offers assessments of work-related injuries, health counseling, referrals to doctors and specialists, and emergency medical response services. The unit also offers programs and counseling on health care and lifestyle.

FBI Headquarters and each of the 56 FBI field offices also maintain a list of available resources for child care. In offices located in or near federal buildings, such care facilities may be on site, although availability may be limited owing to high demand.

The Employee Assistance Program (EAP) is available in all FBI locations and offers assessment, referral, and short-term counseling programs for FBI employees who may be experiencing an adverse event or crisis. The EAP is voluntary and confidential and can deal with psychological, marital, financial, alcohol, or drug-related problems. EAP services are free, although some referral programs may not be. EAP records and operations are protected by federal confidentiality regulations and employees' records are maintained in a secure manner apart from personnel or security files. Participation in an EAP program will not affect an employee's employment or security status.

FBI agents are eligible to enroll in the Federal Employees Health Benefit Program (FEHBP), which permits them to participate in a number of approved health benefit plans, regardless of age or medical condition. The FBI funds part of the cost of participation in these plans, with the agent paying the remainder through automatic payroll deductions. Generally, there are three types of plans available to choose from: the Government-wide Service Benefit Plan (Blue Cross/ Blue Shield), Comprehensive Plans (or health maintenance organizations), and the Employee Organization Plans (fee-for-service plans). In addition, the Special Agents Mutual Benefit Association (SAMBA) offers a plan of its own to all FBI employees. This is considered one of the Employee Organization Plans, but it is not mandatory that agents join it. Some have chosen to go under plans as distant from the FBI as those serving the needs of the U.S. Postal Service. Considering the number and complexity of plans offered, a good bit of homework and comparison shopping may be necessary. Employees have the opportunity to cover themselves, their spouses, and their unmarried dependent children under the age of 22.

Plan selections are for one year only, and agents have the opportunity each year to compare and switch plans during what is called an open season. For many agents this is the only form of health insurance they will ever have, since they are eligible to carry it with them into retirement, with premiums deducted from their pension annuities. For agents who totally retire, it is needed coverage. For agents who become self-employed, it is coverage that will last their lifetime without requiring a physical. Likewise, even retired agents who accept positions in corporations often decline to accept the health coverage offered by those entities, preferring to stay with their government plans. In this manner, if they do not stay with the new private-sector employer long enough to qualify for a pension and lifetime coverage under that health plan, they are assured of uninterrupted coverage under their government plan.

Other Insurance Benefits

All FBI Agents are eligible for coverage under the Federal Employees Group Life Insurance (FEGLI) basic life insurance unless they decide to waive this coverage. The government pays about one-third of the cost of this insurance and the insured amount is the agent's base annual salary, rounded up to the nearest $1,000, plus $2,000. The agent pays the remainder of the premium through a payroll deduction. The basic life package also includes accidental death and dismemberment (ADD) coverage. Employees under the age of 45 are given a no-cost bonus, in that coverage is doubled for employees aged 35 or younger. At age 35 this doubling of coverage begins to be reduced by 10 percent a year until it disappears at age 45, leaving the normal base salary amount as coverage.

Optional coverage under FEGLI can include amounts up to five times the agent's base salary. Spouses and children are also eligible for coverage. In addition, other forms of coverage for agents, spouses, and children are available through SAMBA and also the Special Agents Trust Insurance (SATI). These are paid for by the agent through payroll deductions. While various forms of liability insurance are available, all FBI agents are fully indemnified by the government for all lawful actions taken that are within the scope of their employment.

All FBI employees are eligible for coverage from the Employees Benevolent Fund, which would pay their families $15,000 in the event of their death while employed by the FBI. Special Agents may also participate in the Special Agents Insurance Fund (SAIF), which would pay a $30,000 benefit upon death. Other forms of no-premium insurance, such as the Charles S. Ross Fund and the Public Safety Officers Benefit Fund, also provide special insurance payments in the event an agent is killed in the line of duty.

Another federal program, the Federal Law Enforcement Dependents Assistance Program (FLEDA), will pay college costs for dependents and spouses of federal law-enforcement officers killed or disabled in the line of duty. Expenses covered include tuition, room and board, supplies, and fees.

All FBI agents and employees are also covered by the Federal Employees Compensation Act (FECA), which is a free benefit provided to cover work-related accidents and medical conditions brought on by, or aggravated by, the nature of one's employment. Under FECA the cost of treating the injury or illness can be paid by the U.S. Department of Labor. In addition, a tax-free portion of the agent's salary can be paid if he or she is unable to return to work while recovering.

FBI agents who are sick, injured, or die can expect substantial amounts of unofficial support over and above the programs listed above. This is particularly true if the illness, injury, or death was line-of-duty related. Such support can be emotional, financial, or logistical. Oftentimes, it is all three. By way of example, some years ago a terminally ill agent from Boston was hospitalized at a renown New York City cancer center. New York Office agents, on their own initiative, located suitable and affordable housing for the agent's family close to the hospital, provided transportation assistance to the spouse and family members, and visited the dying agent on a daily basis. They also organized blood-donation drives to lessen the expense of his long and ultimately unsuccessful hospitalization. In the meantime, Boston agents tended to his temporarily vacant house and also assisted family members on that end with transportation and emotional support. Needless to say, agents in both offices helped organize his funeral and assisted the family through that difficult time.

Agents and other FBI employees are also eligible to participate in the Federal Long Term Care Insurance Plan (FLTCIP). This can also cover their spouses, their parents, or their parents-in-law. This program reduces the costs incurred if a covered person needs assistance with daily living activities or has to enter a nursing home, assisted living facility, or hospice. This program is paid for through payroll deductions.

Tax Advantages

Special Agents and other FBI employees are eligible to take advantage of several tax benefits allowed by law. These will have the effect of reducing not only their federal, Social Security, and Medicare taxes but may also reduce state, city, or country taxes. The first of these is the Thrift Savings Plan, discussed above. In addition, since the year 2000, premiums used to pay for federal health insurance programs are likewise exempt from taxation. Beginning in 2003, FBI employees have been able to shelter up to $3,000 each year for health-care costs not covered by their insurance coverage. They may also shelter up to $5,000 each year for child-care and elder-care expenses.

Other Benefits

While an agent is on official travel, the FBI pays all travel-related expenses under a formula used throughout the federal government.

There is, however, a cap on the amount of money that will be paid for food and lodging. Generally, this is not a problem, although it can get a bit tight in major cities and expensive resort locations. However, even in these locales, almost every hotel and motel offers government rates that allow for the per diem caps. If there is no suitable lodging available, there are avenues that an agent can pursue to get the Bureau to grant additional funds.

Agents and other FBI employees are eligible to join the FBI Recreation Association (FBIRA). This is a voluntary, not-for-profit organization that provides recreation opportunities for FBI employees, such as discounted and group tickets to sporting and entertainment events. At some locations, such as FBI Headquarters, Quantico, and some of the larger FBI field offices, it also runs stores that sell FBI clothing, gifts, and memorabilia. The FBIRA also makes this merchandise available through a catalog.

The FBI awards service keys to all its employees. These are awarded at the 10-, 15-, 20-, 25-, 30-, and 35-year levels. Some exceptional support employees serve even longer than 35 years, but no agent does because of the mandatory retirement regulations. The keys come in various shapes and sizes. Most are round with a pendant-type attachment, while the 25-year key is shaped somewhat like the Phi Beta Kappa key. All are gold. Perhaps the most common form of jewelry in the FBI is the 20-year round key, mounted as either a ring for men or a ring or necklace for women. The keys are free; the mounting is paid for by the individual.

What's It Like?

Believe it or not, FBI agents are office workers—at least some of the time. When an agent is assigned to a field office, he or she is also assigned to a squad within that office. This raises an important distinction. The decision of which office an agent is assigned is made by FBI Headquarters; there is no input from the field offices. But once an agent is assigned to an office, the decision as to which squad the agent is assigned is made by the Special Agent in Charge (SAC), with no input from FBI Headquarters. Thus, the new agent coming out of Quantico has two important future events of great personal interest: which office he or she is going to and what squad he or she will be on. This chapter attempts to give you a picture of what being on a field office squad in the FBI will be like.

The Field Office and Squad Assignment

The decision as to which squad an agent is assigned may be based on resource needs, changing priorities of a particular office, or the skill set the individual agent brings to the job. Assuming the agent is not a new arrival from New Agents Training, the squad supervisor normally checks something known as "the book." This is a procedure as old as the FBI itself and really does not involve a book but rather a telephone. The squad supervisor places a call to his or her counterpart for the squad on which the agent served previously. The purpose of the call is to check on the agent's reputation, work habits, skills, strengths, and weaknesses. Depending on the results of that call, the supervisor decides what work the arriving agent will be assigned, the degree of supervision he or she will require, and other administrative issues.

In the case of new agents coming out of Quantico, much the same process is followed but the contact is with an instructor, counselor, or the supervisory special agent in the New Agents Training Unit. Again, questions are asked as to the agent's work ethic, written and oral communications skills, attention to detail, success in practical problems, and the like.

Some large offices have a policy that a newly arrived agent, especially one coming out of training school, is first assigned to the applicant squad for 6 to 12 months. Applicant squads conduct pre-employment and periodic update investigations of persons applying for FBI jobs or candidates for high positions in the federal government. This is done for several reasons. First, it gives the agent time to hone the necessary investigative skills, get his or her feet wet, learn the office routine, and become acquainted with the field office territory. Second, as investigations go, applicant cases are not demanding, so it is a good place for rookies to start. Third, this is a way of spreading the pain, as applicant work is not highly prized by most street agents. New agents are considered, as noted, to be in a probationary agent program for the first 24 months of their time in the Bureau. Failure to perform adequately during this period may be the basis for dismissal, although that is fairly rare. It is more common for the probationary period to be extended, if necessary. Usually, after a period on an applicant squad, an agent is allowed to rotate off to an investigative squad within the office.

Regardless of what squad new agents are assigned to, they will be under the tutelage of a field training agent for the first 12 to 20 months. This reflects the fact that all new agents are considered to have probationary status for the first 24 months of their careers. Those with qualifying prior military service may have probationary status for only 12 months. The field training agent is a more senior agent who acts as both mentor and evaluator of the new arrivals. The supervisory special agent of the squad is also responsible for completing a Probationary Agent Log. This is a checklist of items that the new agents are expected to be exposed to during their probationary periods. For agents assigned to highly specialized squads, the log may be customized so items correspond with the specific line of work. Generally, these items on the log include the normal aspects of a street agent's daily routine, such as making an arrest, appearing in court, writing certain types of communications or reports, or performing complaint duty. Complaint duty is as old as the FBI itself and is the source of many wild and funny stories.

Generally in most FBI field offices, an incoming call or unannounced visitor is directed to the "complaint agent." This is a temporary assignment that is rotated around the office and involves dealing with the public on anything that may be on people's minds. Generally, agents are assigned to complaint duty for a week at a time, after which they return to their squads. Complaint duty can be boring, a nuisance, wildly amusing, or the source of an incredibly important new case. World-class espionage cases, such as the John Walker spy family matter, started with a complaint agent's taking a phone call. Police killings and bank robberies have been solved from information received by complaint agents. On the other hand, practically any FBI agent can recount numbers of "death ray beamed at me by the CIA," "black helicopters following me," or "giant conspiracy to take over the world" stories from some slightly-off-center citizens.

Welcome!

Upon arrival in the new office, the agent is welcomed by the Special Agent in Charge, given a tour of the facility, and offered housing assistance. Once assigned to the squad, the agent may also be assigned a Bureau vehicle, informally known throughout the FBI as a Bucar (pronounced BEW-car). The vehicle is for official business only, although current FBI policy allows agents to use the automobiles to commute to and from their residences, with the caveat that they use the most direct route. The long and the short of this policy is that the vehicles are not to be used for personal business nor are unapproved passengers to be transported in them. A bucar cannot be operated if the driver has had any alcohol. Violations of these regulations can result in swift and harsh punishment, but the availability of a bucar is widely seen as a significant job perk by agents. Gasoline and repairs are paid for by the Bureau, too.

There is a practical aspect to this arrangement. Always using the same vehicle allows agents to carry job-related materials in them, be they photos of suspects or SWAT equipment. Having the vehicle at their homes also means the agents can respond more quickly in the event of an emergency or travel directly from home to a work assignment. Bureau vehicles are normally equipped with an electronic siren, secure radio, and emergency lights. Some vehicles utilized by SWAT or surveillance team members may also have special security devices and storage units for sensitive equipment or shoulder weapons, such as shotguns, rifles, or submachine guns. In offices where it is not possible to assign each agent a vehicle, it is common for two or more agents to share a vehicle, especially if they live in the same general area.

Working Hours and Salary

Agents' work hours are theoretically from 8:15 in the morning until 5:00 at night, but these hours do not include the availability pay hours (discussed in Chapter 2), which average slightly fewer than two hours a day. FBI work is driven substantially by the demands of caseloads and office specials, so in reality most agents wind up working about 10 hours or more a day, on average. This amount of time can vary widely, of course, as some days may be 8½ hours and others 14 hours. The FBI makes reasonable attempts to accommodate the family lives and obligations of its agents, but when there is a conflict, the needs of the FBI always come first. Spousal and family support is essential for anyone in the Special Agent position, for there will inevitably be conflicts between the needs of the Bureau and the needs of family. For example, occasionally there is the need to work nights, weekends, or holidays.

Occasionally, an agent will be required to work shifts—normally to participate in a prolonged surveillance or to help monitor a Title III or court-authorized wiretap. Such assignments typically last from a few weeks to a few months. It is rare for an agent to be assigned to permanent shift work, absent the agent's requesting such an assignment.

Lest one gain the impression that the FBI is an uncaring institution by asking for all this work time, understand that it is not. Families are routinely involved in office social functions, and many offices have special days for agents' kids. The field office is also a source of support during many difficult personal situations; there are countless stories of officemates dipping into their own pockets to help a fellow agent when he or she is faced with family medical emergencies, house fires, and the like. Agents also become friends and often socialize together, as do their families.

The squad to which an agent is assigned will normally have 10 to 15 members with varying degrees of experience. All are "street" agents, meaning they are investigators holding General Service (GS) ratings of 10 to 13. The squad supervisor is a GS-14. The more senior squad members transmit much useful information and learning and will greatly assist newcomers in acclimating. This help could involve providing data on pending cases, input on the tendencies of local federal prosecutors, names of useful informants and their areas of knowledge, insights into relationships with local law-enforcement agencies, the criminal history of the area, and the personality and preferences of the Special Agent in Charge. Items of a more personal nature include information on neighborhoods and schools, good lunch places, fitness clubs, after-hours hangouts, and more. Agents assigned to counterterrorism squads, task forces, or intelligence squads get much the same treatment, but their contacts are with federal, state, and local intelligence groups and agencies. Absent having a prickly personality, the newcomer will quickly be assimilated into the squad and absorb its unique culture within the field office.

Reports and Other Agent Communications

The FBI is a thing of rules and regulations, and these apply to how it communicates and manages cases. An agent carrying a caseload has periodic file reviews with the squad supervisor, during which the supervisor reviews the progress made on each case and offers suggestions for ways to advance it. The supervisor also approves or signs out all communications on the case. These may be periodic reports on case activity made to FBI Headquarters or requests to other field offices for assistance. There are various types and forms of communication in the FBI, and each has its own requirements and format. Learning these will take a new agent a year or so, under the watchful tutelage of the supervisor and field training agent.

Performance Reviews and Transfers

Each agent in the field is given an annual performance review, based on workload and performance in other matters. These reviews are taken quite seriously and can affect promotions, salary increases, and other matters. An agent who is unhappy with a performance review does have an avenue of appeal, but documentation of the basis of the displeasure is required. Agents who are veterans have an additional level of appeal to a government-wide entity, the Merit Systems Protection Board.

After several years' service on one squad and completing the probationary agent program, an agent may request a transfer to another squad in the office, usually for a change of pace or to have the opportunity to learn new skill sets. Within reason, these transfers are normally accommodated. Some agents request a transfer to a resident agency (RA)—a suboffice—either for the chance to work a broader range of cases or to be closer to their residence. These transfers usually go to more senior agents, as RA assignments are often highly prized within most field offices.

Sick Leave and Vacations

Special Agents are, by law, granted 13 sick days a year—enough to cover most illnesses and operations. These days are cumulative, so each year's unused balance rolls forward. Thus, after five or ten years without serious health issues, an agent could be off work for a matter of months and still be drawing full pay. In severe cases, the agent may qualify for a disability retirement from the FBI.

Agents also take vacations, like everyone else. During their first three years of service, agents receive 13 days' vacation time a year. Up to 15 years' service, they receive just under four weeks a year, and after 15 years' service, just over five weeks. Unused vacation time, not to exceed one year's entitlement, can be carried forward from year to year. At the time of retirement or separation from the Bureau, unused vacation days will be paid out to the agent as salary.

The Physical Setting

There is no set design for FBI offices. Many buildings are new, but some are quite old. Generally, each agent has a desk or cubicle, and squad supervisors have private offices. Squads are grouped together in areas informally referred to as "bull pens." The Special Agent in Charge and Assistant Special Agent in Charge have much larger offices, with doors, sofas, and overstuffed chairs. Support personnel are interspersed in the squad areas. These support personnel may include file clerks, word processing personnel, computer technicians, financial analysts, or translators. Increasingly in the FBI, because of the terrorism threat, there also are a significant number of intelligence analysts. There will be a gun vault for the storage of ammunition and shoulder weapons, and also an evidence vault for the maintenance of items of physical evidence. Files are in abundance, as are computers, phones, secure file cabinets, and fax machines. Squads working national security matters and terrorism also have encrypted telephones that permit secure transmission of sensitive information. Identification cards are worn at all times, and holstered firearms and dangling handcuffs are a common sight.

FBI agents in field office assignments normally wear business attire, but they can revert to casual clothes depending on their assignments. For male agents, weapons are worn in hip holsters, riding slightly above the belt and slightly behind the right or left hip bone. Shoulder holsters are frowned upon in the FBI, for safety reasons. Female agents can also wear hip holsters under a suit jacket or sweater, or they can utilize holsters cleverly built into purses or fanny packs. Some agents who have permission to carry a smaller frame weapon of their own choosing use ankle holsters. However, the reality of the situation is that jackets almost always win out, since the weapon is not the only item of equipment many agents carry. If they are on a squad that routinely makes a lot of arrests, such as a bank robbery, fugitive, street gang, or surveillance squad, most agents also carry one or more magazines of ammunition, handcuffs, and perhaps pepper spray or an extendable baton.

Working with Other Agencies

The ability of an agent to relate well to personnel in other agencies is probably a key indicator of his or her ultimate success as a Special Agent. Relationships with state and local law enforcement were, years ago, not one of the FBI's strengths. In many cities, there was a perception that the "locals" were second cousins to the FBI and could often not be trusted with sensitive information. In some isolated instances that may have been true, but all too often the Bureau had a generally condescending attitude toward those in other agencies.

Times have changed. Beginning in the 1970s, the Bureau began to actively court other agencies, as it realized that cooperation was preferable to competition. It was also at this time that the first informal task forces began to appear, in at least some FBI field offices. This shift in attitude, coupled with vastly improved training and selection standards in many law-enforcement agencies, helped level the playing field significantly. Improved cooperation followed shortly thereafter. Today, agents who cannot or will not get along with their state and local counterparts have a tough time succeeding in their work, as much valuable intelligence, criminal and otherwise, is lost.

Cooperation with Federal Prosecutors and Local Police

FBI cooperation with local federal prosecutors is important because agents do not authorize prosecutions. That is done by U.S. Attorneys (USAs) and their assistants, Assistant U.S. Attorneys (AUSAs). The United States is divided into 94 Federal Judicial Districts, each with its own judges and U.S. Attorney. The USAs are political appointees, nominated by the president. The AUSAs are employees of the U.S. Department of Justice and function as the main force behind prosecutorial decisions. The latter are typically young, bright, aggressive lawyers who are the main point of contact for the street agents. AUSAs do not direct investigations, but close collaboration with them is necessary for FBI agents to build strong cases. AUSAs typically serve 6 to 15 years before they are lured away by the much larger salaries offered to them by private law firms, which are attracted to AUSAs because of their vast courtroom experience.

Productive contacts with state and local law-enforcement authorities are also important, since the FBI does not automatically take over an investigation, even a big one. Some crimes are purely federal in nature, while others are purely local and some, called "concurrent jurisdiction," are both local and federal. For example, espionage is purely a federal crime, while murder—absent unusual circumstances—is purely a state and local crime. Some crimes, like bank robberies, are both federal and state and local violations. Under state statutes, a bank robbery is no different from the robbery of a supermarket. But under federal statutes, bank robbery is a federal offense because the bank is insured by the federal government. Because of these issues, there is a premium on sharing resources and intelligence, since there is more than enough work to go around for all concerned.

In areas that involve concurrent jurisdiction, it is not unusual for one agency to hand off a case to another agency. This can be done under the terms of a preexisting Memorandum of Understanding (MOU) between the agencies or on an ad hoc, informal basis. For example, in one city it may be routine for the FBI to handle bank robbery cases, but in an instance in which a police officer was killed or wounded during the bank robbery, a decision may be made to shift the case to local authorities for prosecution. The investigation of the matter would still be a joint effort, but the local authorities and community would have the satisfaction of handling a matter that had deeply affected one of their own. In other instances, local authorities may hand a matter off to the FBI, since the federal penalties for the crimes are more severe than those under state statutes.

The above distinctions may be confusing to some people, who have heard news reports about FBI involvement in a local murder case. While murder is almost always a state and local offense, the FBI does get involved in such matters under a number of conditions. The first of these could be if there's been a request from a state or local agency for assistance. Second, if the perpetrator of the crime has been charged locally and is believed to have fled, state or local authorities may request the FBI to get federal charges filed under the Unlawful Flight to Avoid Prosecution (UFAP) statute. This allows the FBI to search for the subject throughout the United States and the world. Third, if the person who committed the crime was tried and convicted but escaped, the FBI could be asked to file federal charges under the Unlawful Flight to Avoid Confinement (UFAC) statute, which again would allow the Bureau to search for the fugitive. In the past several decades, the role of the FBI in UFAP and UFAC matters has dwindled somewhat, as some of these responsibilities were taken over by the U.S. Marshal's Service. Even so, at any given time the Bureau is seeking about 12,000 fugitives, most of them charged with the most serious felony offenses.

The Role of Task Forces

Many, if not most, field offices now have task forces within them. Larger field offices may have a dozen or more. These are cooperative efforts of the FBI to team with other federal agencies, state, and local law-enforcement personnel to address crime problems in their area. Task forces can be formed to handle bank robberies, terrorism, narcotics cartels, street gangs, or serial killers. Task force members operate as a squad within the office. All non-FBI personnel assigned to task forces undergo full field background investigations, have top secret clearances, and have full access to FBI files and data systems. Given the often tight budgets of many state and local agencies, the FBI often provides cars, radios, and other support for task force members from other agencies.

One of the effects of the events of 9/11 was to restructure the squad composition of FBI field offices. Prior to that day, intelligence squads working national security matters (NSM) were found in all large FBI offices—and many medium-sized ones, as well—as were Joint Terrorism Task Forces (JTTF) squads. Now all FBI field offices have at least one NSM squad and one JTTF squad.

The Extensive FBI Resources

One of the most important aspects of an FBI field office is not actually in the office: indexes. At one time, these were little more than 3 by 5 cards, maintained in scores, if not hundreds, of file cabinets in every FBI field office. For example, the New York Office of the FBI had over 7 million such cards before the system was automated. The FBI has long prided itself on information management, and under Director Hoover, the development of the index system was a notable first for the FBI. The Bureau has many complex rules about indexing, and laborious though it may be, it is one of the most important things an agent does. If, for example, an agent conducts an interview of a witness to a bank robbery, the person's name, address, and phone number are indexed. So, too, are the names and information developed during the course of the interview. This indexing is now done on a computer system, so that all FBI field offices share the same information. If, years later, only the phone number came up in another investigation, it could be traced back to the original interview. Indeed, many cases have been made or advanced over the years through the ability of the FBI to retrieve information from its own files.

New agents will probably spend the first days or even weeks reading case files and informant reports to catch up on the history of existing cases. Then they will begin the work of being agents, developing a work plan to advance the cases to which they are assigned. To some degree these steps will be discussed informally with the squad supervisor. The work then begins and could consist of conducting interviews, meeting with local law enforcement and federal prosecutors, contacting informants, coordinating surveillances, or requesting investigative assistance from other FBI field offices. Depending on the nature of the case load and the manner in which the agent chooses to pursue it, the agent may then develop a pattern of being in the office seldom or on a regular basis. There is, however, an old saying in the FBI: "You don't solve them in the office." This reflects the age-old consensus in law enforcement that the best use of one's time is being on the street, talking to people and asking questions.

The Types of Cases the FBI Agent Handles

Generally there are three types of cases within the FBI: small, medium, and large. These are terms never used within the Bureau to describe an investigation, but are a convenient way to introduce some examples of FBI jurisdiction and activity. A brief examination of each type provides some working idea of what life as an FBI agent is like.

Small Cases

A small case may be a relatively minor violation, such as a crime aboard an aircraft, known as a CAB. In the case of a hijacking, this would be considered a major case, however most of these involve an unruly or drunken passenger giving the flight crew a hard time. Usually, persons who fall into this category are arrested by local airport police upon the aircraft's arrival at its destination and held until the FBI shows up. The Bureau first checks with the local AUSA to see if the prosecutor is willing to authorize prosecution. By authorizing prosecution, the AUSA is saying, in effect, "If you investigate this and substantiate what we think happened, I am willing to take it to trial."

In an instance like this, the agents would take the prisoner into federal custody, search, fingerprint, and photograph him, and interview him. The prisoner would then be taken before a U.S. Magistrate for a preliminary hearing, which could result in being released on bond or returned to confinement. The agents would also interview the members of the flight crew who dealt with the person and also any passengers who may have been witnesses to the event. They would then write up their report, provide it the AUSA, and conduct any additional investigation the AUSA might believe is necessary. If the matter later goes to trial, the agents would appear to testify and also introduce evidence.

Medium Cases

A bank robbery is a good example of a *medium* case in terms of complexity, but it offers a platform to introduce almost the full range of FBI Special Agent duties. For example, the FBI is normally notified of a bank robbery by the local police or an alarm company servicing the bank. Agents respond, using lights and sirens, and secure the crime scene. Witnesses are located and segregated. This is important, as there is often a human tendency to compare notes about what just happened and arrive at a consensus story. This is not an attempt to deceive, but rather a human behavior to make sense of a highly unusual event.

A "neighborhood" is conducted to ascertain if there are persons in the area or on the street who might have seen or heard something of value. By this point the police have broadcast a description, as best they have it, of the subjects and the getaway car. One group of agents begins to interview the witnesses, one at a time. The FBI never does group interviews, since human beings have the tendency to influence each other and one witness's account may shade or overshadow that of another witness. Another group of agents begins to process the crime scene, looking for fingerprints, cartridge cases, and projectiles if shots were fired, or items the robbers may have dropped. Still a third group of agents is handling the "bait money," which is prerecorded currency that tellers are trained to provide in the case of a robbery. The serial numbers of these bills are entered in the National Crime Information Center (NCIC) computer as quickly as possible, in case the offenders have been apprehended some distance away by police unfamiliar with the robbery. If these officers find a large quantity of cash, they run it through NCIC to see if it is connected to a crime. These agents also work with bank management to determine the amount of the loss.

Still other agents work with the bank and their security provider to access photos of the robbery. In most banks, when an alarm button is hit or bait money is removed from a drawer, various systems begin to video-record the scene. Owing to advances in technology and the relative cheapness of digital recording equipment, some banks have their floors and working areas under video surveillance at all times, not just when an alarm has been triggered. These photos are copied and distributed to all agents in the field office and might also be provided to local news outlets for broadcast in the hope of generating leads as to the identities of the perpetrators. In some localities there are tipster programs that offer rewards for information provided confidentially about crimes and wanted persons, and these may also be utilized.

Finally, other agents work with the local police to ascertain what they know of the robbery and who they believe might be likely suspects. It is not uncommon for the getaway car in bank robberies to be found by local police within a mile or two of the bank, usually indicating a switch car was used to get away from the bank. Since the first car was likely stolen, agents are dispatched to the scene of that theft to develop any information as to who might have stolen it. The switch car is then processed by agents, again looking for fingerprints or any other productive evidence. A "neighborhood" is again conducted, as there is always the chance that someone may have seen the robbers switch from one vehicle to another. In an era of video surveillance, local shops and residences might be contacted to determine if there were surveillance cameras in operation and if they were positioned to pick up the switching of vehicles.

At the beginning of the investigation, the squad supervisor designates one agent as the case agent, meaning the individual is responsible for the investigation until it is concluded. This agent must tie all this concurrent activity together and determine the next steps. The case agent is also responsible for all written reports on the case and setting out the leads, which are requests for assistance from other FBI field offices. When the leads are set out, in FBI parlance, the office that has the case is called the office of origin and the office supporting the investigation is called the auxiliary office.

Assuming the robbers are not apprehended fairly quickly or turned in by a tipster from a television broadcast, the work of the case agent begins in earnest. The individual circulates the description of the robbery and the photos to surrounding FBI offices and law-enforcement agencies in the hope that someone will either recognize the persons in the photos or the modus operandi (MO) used in the robbery. Many perpetrators are career criminals and return to a life of crime when released from prison. Most also do not move great distances from home, so it is always possible that someone who has arrested them before will recognize them again. Likewise, some criminals fall into patterns of behavior when they commit their crimes, and it is possible another law-enforcement officer will recognize some odd or pronounced element of the crime and tie it to a technique the officer has seen before.

The case agent also begins to check informants and other sources of information who might have knowledge of the robbers' activities. When one or more suspects is developed through this process, the case agent then requests the Criminal Justice Information Services Division of the FBI to check their fingerprints on file against those of value recovered at the scene. Also, with the development of suspects, the case agent may return to show witnesses a photo spread of the suspects' photos intermingled with those of other criminals not involved in this robbery. From such spreads one or more witnesses may choose the perpetrators of the robbery.

As the investigation proceeds, the case agent provides periodic reports to FBI Headquarters and also to the U.S. Attorney's Office. If the case agent and the AUSA believe they are zeroing in on the likely perpetrators of the robbery, they may go before a Grand Jury and try to get a "true bill," or indictment. In other instances, they may go before a federal judge to obtain a bench warrant, based on convincing the judge that they have developed probable cause to charge certain individuals with this robbery.

With the issuance of warrants for arrest (called "paper" by most law-enforcement agencies), the case then becomes a fugitive investigation. Now the identities of the perpetrators are known; only their location is not. Conducting the fugitive investigation involves many elements used in the initial bank robbery investigation. Names and identifying data are entered into the NCIC computer database; wanted flyers are sent to FBI offices and other law-enforcement agencies; the media may be enlisted to publicize the names, photos, and descriptions of the fugitives; informants are contacted to see if they have information of value; relatives and former criminal associates are questioned to see if they have information of value; banks are alerted in the event the fugitives are spotted casing another bank. There might also be fixed surveillances of addresses or locations where the fugitives are known to hang out or there may be moving surveillances of their friends, family, or associates.

These processes continue until the bank robbers are caught. This might take years, or in some instances may never occur, although about 85 percent of all bank robbers are eventually caught.

When the fugitives are taken into custody, the job of the case agent is in many ways just beginning, for now the individual must prepare for trial. The agent works closely with the AUSA, organizes evidence, conducts follow-up investigations, contacts witnesses, arranges fingerprint or scientific testimony if needed, and remains alert to the possibility that one or more of the subjects may "reach out" to the case agent. It is not unusual for criminals, in custody and facing trial, to try to cut deals by informing on other criminals. The case agent normally is the conduit through which criminals initiate this process, but the negotiation must be closely coordinated with the AUSA assigned to the case and also the defense counsel for the accused.

Major Cases

A classic example of a *major* case is the investigation of a mob family. This could be generated from an informant tip, input from local police, items overheard in a wiretap on another case, a mobster looking to help his situation when facing a long sentence for a crime, information received from foreign authorities, tips coming out of an FBI undercover operation or perhaps one run by another law-enforcement agency, complaints from a business or entire industry tired of being extorted and exploited, or some mixture of one or more of these elements. The initiation of such a case requires considerable study by the SAC, consultation with FBI Headquarters, and discussions with the USA, since one or more squads may be involved on a full-time basis for several years.

For example, various groups on the squad or squads will be involved in reviewing past intelligence files and informant reports or in listening again to tapes from wiretaps not previously believed to be related. Other agents may visit foreign countries to gain a better understanding of the information possessed by those authorities. Massive amounts of surveillance time may be scheduled as agents begin to track and understand the hierarchy and operations of the group in question. Often, this surveillance involves the use of aircraft. Frequently, the surveillance target may travel to a distant state, requiring coordination and planning with one or more other FBI field offices. Other agents will be tasked with attempting to develop informants likely to be in positions to provide intelligence of value. When there is probable cause, applications will be made for Title III wiretaps and, perhaps, the installation of closed-circuit television coverage. Once in place, these installations have to be monitored 24 hours a day for perhaps years. The agents working on the wire have to practice the demanding art of "minimization," a requirement handed down by the federal courts that stipulates that only those portions of a conversation that relate to or appear to relate to criminal activity can be recorded.

Another group of agents performs the laborious and largely thankless task of completing all of the paperwork required by FBI and Department of Justice policy, and also detailed in court decisions, as to how wiretaps are recorded, logged, duplicated, transcribed, stored, and treated. Still other agents are tasked with providing contact and cover for informants and cooperating witnesses (CW) who may travel throughout the United States and the world in support of the investigation. A CW is a person who has some relationship with the target group but is not believed to be a major player. Oftentimes, these persons are convinced that it is their best long-term interests to be on the side of the good guys. They may report back on the target group and its members, record consensual telephone conversations, or wear a wire on their body. Some agents on the investigation deal with technical specialists at FBI Headquarters who will work with these tapes to filter and remove static and background noise. Still other agents may travel abroad to help foreign authorities coordinate arrests in their countries that will advance the investigation.

The demands of major task-force investigations are so great and so complex that in some instances one agent is detailed to act as a scheduler and coordinator for other agents' travel and work assignments. Even as agents are working on an investigation that might span three to five years, vacations are taken, illnesses occur, training is received, the requirement for firearms qualification does not go away, and kids get sick. Coordinating so large an undertaking involving so many specialties is no small task.

FBI support personnel play a number of significant roles in so large and lengthy an investigation. Word processing personnel listen to perhaps thousands of hours of tape-recorded conversations, replaying them many times to ensure they are accurately transcribing what is on the tapes, which are often full of the coarsest language imaginable. When they are done, agents then have to sit for countless hours comparing those transcripts to the tapes to ensure their accuracy. Still other support personnel (financial analysts) assist Special Agent accountants in the effort to map the financial infrastructure of the family and chart its business dealings. Intelligence analysts study the details of the investigation to seek patterns, tendencies, and possible links to other persons and groups. Still other support personnel provide language translation services or process and enhance surveillance photographs. Others enter daily updates into special mapping software programs designed to provide a hierarchical picture of the family and the relationships within it.

At each step of the investigation, continuing assessments have to be made as to what techniques seem to be most productive, which targets are the most likely to be candidates for criminal prosecution, how accurate and comprehensive informant coverage is, if persons have been identified who might be receptive to development as new informants, if new players of significance are being identified, and if the range of the group's criminal activities is broader or deeper than expected. All of these factors may cause the investigation to expand or contract for shift direction or emphasis.

Indeed, it is not uncommon for such investigations to become international in scope fairly quickly, which may require agents to work closely with the local U.S. Attorney's office and also attorneys at the Department of Justice (referred to usually as Main Justice) to craft and effect international warrants, extraditions, and other procedures in the criminal justice process. Likewise, it is also not unusual for two or more criminal investigations to bump into each other. Given that some of these criminal enterprises are huge, it is likely some other federal, state, or local agency is also investigating some element of it. When this occurs there may be a brief turf fight, but usually these situations result in two, three, or more agencies coming to work together to achieve the dismantling of the group.

When one of these investigations is concluded—or "brought down," in law-enforcement parlance—much work is still to be done. Mobsters have access to high-priced legal counsel and mob trials can be lengthy and complicated. As the government prepares its case, there will be additional investigations to be conducted and, usually, deals to be considered, since mobsters also watch out for themselves before their allegiance to their "family." Witnesses may have to be relocated or even entered into the Witness Protection Program to ensure their safety. Search warrants may have to be drawn up and executed to secure evidence that could consist of a murder weapon, a stash of stolen goods, or even one or more bodies of mob victims buried long ago.

The successful conclusion of so long and complicated an investigation is the conviction of all the subjects of the investigation in court. When this happens, as one might suspect, a large party occurs. Lifelong bonds may form on task forces and between investigators and prosecutors, since they have lived in the crucible of this investigation for many years and have seen it through its ups and downs and twists and turns. The success is sweet, but the costs are not inconsiderable.

Special Skills for Solving Special Crimes

It should be noted that the above examples all involve criminal cases. The FBI has equally diverse categories of cases in three other fields: counterintelligence, counterterrorism, and intelligence. Indeed, at present the FBI is considering a somewhat more formal approach to the career development of field office investigative agents, or "street agents" as they are known in the Bureau. This is a marked departure from traditional FBI thinking, and it seeks to recognize that different skill sets and developmental experiences are required in the four major lines of FBI investigative activity. The idea is to document the career progression believed to produce the "ideal" investigator in each line of work, then attempt to structure agents' career progression so as to provide them with the needed developmental experiences. The concept, while sound, is subject to vigorous debate within the FBI. On the one hand, the need for specialized expertise is recognized if the FBI is to succeed in demanding new areas of responsibility, such as counterterrorism. On the other hand, segmenting agents by investigative specialty also tends to reduce the flexibility needed to shift to new duties as needs arise. At this point, the FBI still has the concept under review.

The Dangers of the Job

An FBI agent, whether newly out of training school or a 25-year veteran, lives in a world that is different in many ways from that of his or her fellow citizens. One of the first differences is danger.

A substantial amount of time is spent in training school on firearms and defensive tactics training. There is a reason for this. Criminals are dangerous people and when the agent is confronted, his or her priorities are, in order: don't get hurt, don't let any innocent bystander get hurt, don't let the bad guy get hurt. If the bad guy has to be hurt, or even killed, so be it if that is necessary, but it is not a desirable outcome. In this regard, the FBI has a substantial advantage over state and local law enforcement. The vast majority of injuries and deaths in law-enforcement work come as a result of unplanned encounters. These could be police officers coming upon a robbery in progress, responding to a burglary call, attempting to break up a domestic dispute, seeking to enforce a court order, or stopping a vehicle for a traffic violation. Even though they receive the best training and equipment possible, state and local officers almost always work at the disadvantage of not knowing who or what they are dealing with. The vehicle they just stopped could be driven by a middle-aged executive with no criminal history or someone fresh out of prison with a gun and a grudge.

The FBI, on the other hand, almost always has time, resources, and planning on its side. If a dangerous fugitive is to be arrested, it is rarely on the spur of the moment. The FBI works to carefully plan, staff, and time the arrest to give the fugitive as little chance to resist as possible. Things can go wrong and people, even the good people, do get hurt and killed, but the odds are vastly in the agents' favor. In its history, the FBI has lost 34 agents to hostile fire in the line of duty, a fair number of them in the gangster days of the 1930s. The most recent death was in 2001. The made-for-TV movie *In The Line of Duty: The FBI Murders* is an excellent and accurate depiction of one of the bloodiest days in FBI history, when two FBI agents were killed and a number of others seriously wounded in a running gun battle with two heavily armed bank robbers in Miami in the 1980s.

In addition to the agents who lost their lives to hostile fire, 14 others died in the performance of a law-enforcement duty. These tragic deaths could have occurred during a training exercise, in car crashes while on duty, or in aircraft crashes while training or conducting a surveillance.

Undercover Work

Although it is not part of the career development program, some agents volunteer for service as an undercover agent (UCA). All UCAs are volunteers, and there is no special compensation for performing these duties. Generally, UCAs must have a solid investigative background before being considered for such work and also receive the full support of their superiors. Their undercover activities may take place in the office territory to which they are assigned or another field office many miles away. Volunteers for this program are evaluated for their expertise and psychological suitability. Special training programs are also available at Quantico to teach agents the tricks of pulling off an undercover assignment.

The vast majority of undercover operations are criminal in nature, but intelligence-directed undercover operations also take place. Generally, undercover assignments fall into one of two categories. Group II undercover operations can be approved by the Special Agent in Charge, with the concurrence of the local U.S. Attorney. Group IIs, as they are called, still require careful coordination and planning, but generally they are less sensitive, less dangerous, of shorter term, and less costly than other types of operations. Group I undercover operations are the opposite. They may be dangerous, elaborate, lengthy, technically challenging, involving prominent personages, be very costly, or have foreign aspects involved. Group Is require painstaking planning, substantial amounts of documentation, lots of coordination, and minute review by a panel of senior FBI Headquarters and Department of Justice officials. Perhaps the most legendary FBI Group I undercover operation was ABSCAM, a political corruption investigation that resulted in the conviction of members of Congress in the 1980s. Probably the most well known Group I operation was that of Special Agent Joe Pistone, who infiltrated the La Cosa Nostra (Mafia) with devastating results to the mobsters. So successful was Pistone in his role that he carried it out for years and was on the verge of becoming a "made guy" when the operation was terminated. His exploits were recounted in the book and movie that bears his undercover name, *Donnie Brasco*.

Agents serving as a UCA may be in either a light or deep cover role. Those in a light cover capacity, generally those involved in Group IIs, may have little disruption to their normal routine and family lives. Those in Group I operations may be in very deep cover and may be away from their families for extended periods. They may also be required to adopt a foreign persona for an extended time, posing as a drug dealer, crooked businessman, hit man, terrorist, or stock swindler.

Owing to the personal and psychological risks associated with all undercover operations, but especially deep-cover Group Is, each UCA active in an undercover operation has a contact agent for the duration of the operation. This contact agent is the UCA's link to the real world and serves a number of roles. The contact agent can relay messages to family and friends, can provide physical and psychological support, can be available in times of danger, and is also charged with continually evaluating the physical and psychological health of the UCA. At any sign of deterioration or excess danger, the UCA is extracted from the operation, even if this means shutting it down. Perhaps the best evidence of the amount of thought and planning the FBI puts into its undercover operations is the fact that in the face of tremendous danger and some ticklish situations, only one FBI agent has been killed while working in an undercover capacity.

Working with Informants

Danger can come in many forms for an agent, and one of them is definitely a mixed blessing—informants. Generally, there are two types of informants in the FBI: criminal (137s) and counterintelligence (134s). They are often referred to by their numbers, which is how they are designated in the FBI's case numbering system. An agent, thus, might say, "I have to meet my 137 at 7:30."

Informants are a mixed bag. A good one can make the agent a star, can make the field office look good, and indeed can reflect positively on the entire FBI. Great informants have been instrumental in many FBI successes over the years. It was an informant who provided the information that initiated and sustained the multiyear ABSCAM political corruption investigation. Likewise, an informant was crucial to the FBI's locating the bodies of the three slain civil-rights workers near Philadelphia, Mississippi, in the 1960s. On the intelligence side, the number of FBI informants in the Communist Party USA in the 1950s and 1960s was so great that it neutralized the ability of that organization to cause serious problems for the United States and also became the staple of more than a few stand-up comedy routines. And in this age of terrorism, the value of an informant is obvious. The ability to disrupt and head off potentially devastating terrorist incidents is crucial to the success of the FBI's new mission.

Informants can save the Bureau untold hours of time, money, and effort. They can finger suspects; locate fugitives; identify unknown persons; provide advance notice of future criminal, intelligence, or terrorist activity; help map the organizational structure of a group; locate stolen goods, safe houses, or hideous activities; divulge methods of communication among group members; and facilitate the introduction of undercover agents into a gang. They can report on power struggles within a group and also identify others who, for various reasons, might also be recruited as new informants. Informants do not operate out of the goodness of their hearts. Some want money, and truly exceptional informants may be paid substantial sums. Others want a long-term relationship with the FBI as a sort of insurance policy in case they get caught while involved in criminal activity themselves. The FBI does not "license" or condone criminal acts by an informant, but it is also realistic enough to understand that informants come by their first-hand knowledge of the underworld only by being very closely associated with it themselves. Few informants are choirboys.

Other informants want to settle grudges against fellow criminals or try to help themselves when facing substantial criminal charges. Some merely seek to eliminate their competition by setting them up for arrest. Often they are shrewd, street-smart, and tough negotiators. Also, having survived a life on the streets, they are often excellent judges of character and personality and are skillful manipulators. Intelligence informants, called "assets," cooperate for many of the same reasons, although a few act mainly or solely on ideological grounds, often at great personal risk.

There is an old saw in the Bureau that has much truth: Never fall in love with an informant. This is hard-earned wisdom distilled through the ages, for many times in both criminal and counterintelligence operations agents have come to grief because of informants. This can take many forms. On a few occasions, agents have literally fallen in love with an informant, in the romantic sense. Little good comes of this. Several decades ago a married agent went to prison when it was learned that he had murdered his informant/lover lest she disclose their relationship to his wife.

Other agents have come to be too close to informants, treating them as friends. That this happens is not as unusual as some might think. The agent sees and appreciates what the informant is going through and the risks the individual is taking, ostensibly on the agent's behalf. The agent and the informant may spend substantial time together during debriefing sessions. Some come to actually like the informant, despite their rough nature and checkered past. Many informants are bright, colorful characters with endless stories to tell and a taste for the good life. But palling around with an informant can quickly get out of hand. As noted, some informants are master manipulators and try to position the agent so they can extract information from them, ostensibly to assist them in their attempts to better serve the agent's interests. Still other informants have lent agents money, which is against a number of FBI rules, as a token of friendship or to have a psychological lever over the agent.

Whatever the issue, informants are a reason for concern and caution. Good agents often have good informants, but even the best and most productive must always be wary of becoming too close. Because of the many issues surrounding informants, and also because of public concerns about possible intrusiveness by a federal agency, all FBI informant operations are governed by attorney general guidelines.

Weapons and Weapons Skills

Discussions of danger bring to mind the matter of weapons. There is no requirement that an FBI agent carry a weapon off duty, but almost all do. Oftentimes it is their duty weapon, but many agents choose to carry a smaller, more concealable weapon during off-duty hours. Their choice is not unlimited, however. The Bureau publishes a list of approved weapons and calibers from which agents may choose. The purchase of the weapon is, however, at the agent's expense. Once an alternative, approved weapon has been purchased, it may also be carried on duty in lieu of the Bureau-issued service weapon. Some street agents do this, but most do not, preferring the greater firepower and accuracy of their service weapon while performing street work. As they move into more administrative, managerial, or support roles, many agents substitute their off-duty weapon for their service weapon.

Agents must pass a firearms proficiency test four times a year. A passing score is 80, firing from a variety of positions, using both hands at once, and using each hand separately. If agents cannot pass a test, they will be given opportunities to take make-up tests. Continued failure to pass a firearms test will result in agents being placed on limited duty and, in extreme cases, in termination from the FBI. An agent who has one or more Bureau-approved personal weapons must also qualify with them, which can present problems. Smaller frame and shorter barrel weapons, while lighter and more concealable, are also more difficult to fire accurately.

The requirement to be able to fire accurately with either hand reflects both practical considerations and FBI philosophy. The practical aspect is that one hand or arm may be hit during a gun battle, requiring the agent to switch the weapon to the other hand. The philosophical aspect involves the FBI's belief in the use of cover and concealment. In all FBI firearms training, agents are taught to use any available cover. On the street this could be a parked car, telephone pole, fire hydrant, mailbox, or corner of a building. Depending on the location of the adversary and the location of the available cover, it may be necessary to fire the weapon with the nondominant, "weak" hand.

Agents are authorized to carry their weapon anywhere within the United States, to include airliners, after proper forms have been completed, but they cannot consume alcoholic beverages while armed on such flights. In airlines terms, armed law enforcement personnel on aircraft are called LEOs (Law Enforcement Officers). When the paperwork is done, one copy of the form goes to the pilot of the aircraft, one copy to the chief flight attendant, and the agent keeps the third. Some agents make it a practice to introduce themselves to the pilot so they will know what they look like in the event of an incident on the aircraft. Other agents also ask if there are any other LEOs on the flight, so in the event of an incident the good guys know who is who. Absent unusual circumstances, agents are not permitted to carry their weapons outside the United States.

Weapons are a permanent facet of an agent's life, and this is where safety becomes an issue. The FBI has no tolerance for the unsafe handling of any firearm, on or off duty, and this theme is repeated throughout firearms training. Agents must also allow for the fact that they will be taking their weapons home every evening. Some agents lock their weapons in a secure location while others buy special locks available in gun shops to render the weapons inoperable. Most agents have families, and kids and firearms are not a good combination, so many err on the side of caution.

For single agents, weapons also pose some interesting problems. When in social settings such as parties, restaurants, or bars, many agents are less than forthcoming about their employment. Some may say that they work for the government. Others will tell half the truth—if they are lawyers, they may simply say they are lawyers and not mention the fact that they are also FBI agents. Some are even less forthcoming than that. Should a dating relationship develop out of such encounters, the weapons problem becomes prominent fairly quickly. Agents have the choice of going out on dates unarmed or carrying their weapons and hoping they don't get noticed. Obviously, as the frequency or depth of a relationship increases, the weapon will probably get discovered. There are many funny stories in the FBI about such moments.

Rewards and Penalties

A discussion of informants is perhaps a logical place to begin to consider two other matters related often to informants and informant operations: rewards and penalties. The FBI has longstanding employee recognition and employee disciplinary programs that apply to all facets of FBI operations and to both Special Agent and support personnel.

The most basic FBI reward is a *letter of commendation*. This is proposed at the FBI field office or Headquarters division level and must be approved by the Administrative Services Division at FBI Headquarters, along with any other division having an interest in the matter at hand. This letter is sent to the employee's boss for presentation, and a copy is placed in the individual's Headquarters and field personnel files. The next highest award is an *incentive award*, which is a letter of commendation with a cash payment. These payments may range from several hundred dollars to well over a thousand dollars. In addition there are award programs that involve the presentation of medals to deserving employees.

In the last two decades, the FBI also instituted a program of recognition that had been in effect for many years at other law-enforcement and intelligence agencies. The FBI's *Honorary Medals Program* was instituted to supplement, not replace, the existing system of letters of commendation and incentive awards, and was intended to afford deserving employees a tangible remembrance of their extraordinary deeds. The program includes the following medals:

- *FBI Star.* This medal is awarded for serious physical injury suffered in the direct line of duty in physical confrontation with an adversary.
- *FBI Medal for Meritorious Achievement.* This medal is awarded for extraordinary and exceptional achievement in a duty of extreme challenge and great responsibility. It is also awarded for extraordinary and exceptional actions in a criminal or national security matter involving decisive, exemplary acts that result in the protection or saving of lives.
- *Memorial Star.* This medal is awarded to the next of kin of an FBI employee who lost his or her life as a result of line-of-duty actions involving a direct adversary.

- *Shield of Bravery.* This medal is awarded for brave and coura-geous acts occurring in the line of duty or within the scope of FBI employment. The acts may be committed in the context of a task force operation, undercover operation, or grave or crisis situations.

- *Medal of Valor.* This medal is presented for exceptional acts of heroism or voluntary risk of life and personal safety in the direct line of duty and involving and in the face of criminal adver-saries.

FBI employees are also eligible for Department of Justice award pro-grams. These programs cover all employees, attorneys, and law-enforcement officers within the department.

At the other end of the spectrum are the disciplinary procedures of the FBI. The least serious form of discipline is a *letter of censure*. This is a written reprimand, proposed by either the field office or the Headquarters division and approved by the Administrative Services Division and perhaps other Headquarters' divisions. The letter of cen-sure is placed into the employee's Headquarters and field personnel files and may negatively affect promotions and other actions for a period of a year or more.

The next most serious form of punishment is a letter of censure *and being placed on probation* for several months or even a year or more. Being in a probationary status means that if the employee is involved in another infraction of FBI rules and regulations the effect of that misdeed will be magnified. In FBI terms, censure and proba-tion is referred to as a "two bagger."

More serious than censure and probation is censure, probation, *and suspension without pay*. The period of suspension may range from one week to four weeks. Personnel having received such discipline will be in major trouble if they err again while on probation. In the field, if an agent is popular and the offense was deemed unfortunate but not grossly derelict, it is common for other agents to chip in to help the offending agent recover the lost salary.

The next most serious form of punishment is censure, probation, suspension, *and a disciplinary transfer to another location.* All the above factors pertain to this punishment, with the significant addition of the agent and his or her family being uprooted. Even though the FBI will pay for this transfer, it is a major setback to both the agent and the family. The movement of the agent and family might be seen as needlessly draconian. But it is the Bureau's position that transfer is necessary since the offending behavior was so egregious that the effectiveness of the agent in that office and in the local law-enforcement community may well have been compromised. It is unusual for support personnel to receive this form of punishment. As might be expected, the two forms of punishment above are referred to as "three baggers" and "four baggers."

Obviously, the most serious form of punishment is *dismissal from the FBI.* This punishment is very carefully reviewed by FBI Headquarters before being applied, but it is used in extreme cases of disciplinary lapses.

Lest a discussion of such issues imply that the FBI and its agents are rouge elephants on a rampage, it should be noted that most agents make it through a 20- or 25-year career without so much as a letter of censure. Perhaps 10 or 15 percent will receive a latter of censure at some point for a minor infraction. More serious forms of punishment are relatively rare.

The Personal and the Private

Lifestyle is an issue that brings out differences consistent with FBI service. The FBI has no interest in one's personal or sexual life as long as behavior is not illegal or immoral. It is the latter word that brings disagreements to the fore. The FBI and some small number of its agents have struggled over the years, sometimes to the point of litigation, as to what is reasonable and acceptable. There is, and will be, ongoing discussion and disputes as to what is legitimately one's personal business and what the FBI can reasonably and legally expect of a government employee who holds a top secret clearance, carries a weapon, and has the power of arrest. (All FBI agents and support employees hold top secret clearances even if they are not assigned to counterintelligence or terrorism investigations.) The FBI's argument is that if the public, whose cooperation is essential to accomplish the FBI mission, does not hold agents (and their lifestyles) in high regard, their assistance may not be as readily forthcoming.

Domestic issues can and do occur, as agents are human beings like everyone else. Normal domestic disagreements and even divorces happen, but problems like domestic violence may bring involvement by the Bureau, sanctions on the agent, and in serious cases, dismissal.

Alcohol use is another area that has brought more than a few agents to grief. Normal, social alcohol consumption is fine, but any agent who receives a Driving While under the Influence (DWI) citation, on or off duty, will face serious disciplinary sanctions from the FBI. Attempts to use one's position and credentials to convince a police officer to overlook a citation or arrest is another sure way to bring down the wrath of the Bureau. The use of illegal drugs is strictly prohibited.

Many years ago the FBI recognized that alcohol use could be a problem with agents, as it has been for law enforcement in general. The Bureau created the Employee Assistance Program, with trained representatives in every FBI office, to offer counseling and support in a confidential, nonpunitive manner. The program is available for any other legitimate problem, such as family crises or the onset of psychological problems.

One's weight is also subject to interest by the FBI. The FBI maintains desirable weight standards for agents, adjusted for height and sex. The theory is that agents' job descriptions require them to be capable of vigorous physical activities. Excessive weight is considered detrimental to that job requirement, so if an agent returning from his or her annual physical is well beyond the weight range, the individual may be required to embark upon a program to reduce the poundage. Exceptions are permitted for medical and physical conditions, but disciplinary actions may wait for those unable or unwilling to shed the needed pounds.

Physical examinations raise other problems as well. Agents are required to take periodic physicals, depending on their age. This frequency may vary from once every three years for those under 33 years of age to once a year for those over 33 years. In addition, after age 40, agents are given a stress test biannually. The physicals are paid for by the FBI and often take place at governmental facilities. People change with time and age, and not all these changes are for the good. Conditions may be discovered that will affect an agent's ability to perform the full range of duties. The results of the physical are shared with the agent and also are reviewed at FBI Headquarters by the chief medical officer. In most instances, the FBI is more than accommodating to work with agents to resolve these conditions, adjust duty schedules, and take other actions to keep the agent fully and productively employed. In extreme cases it may be necessary to put the agent in a Limited Duty status, further restricting duties and opportunities. In some rare cases, it is necessary to process the agent for a disability pension, even if this is against the individual's wishes.

The FBI requires that its agents maintain themselves in good physical shape, and in the past there were periodic physical fitness tests administered in the field offices. In recognition that this is a legitimate job requirement, the FBI does allow agents to take time out of their workdays to work out, either singly or in groups. The current allotment for such activities is three hours a week.

Potential Conflicts of Interest

Finances and business issues raise further distinctions between the agent population and the general public. Agents are not allowed to have outside employment or be active participants in outside businesses. Those considering an FBI career who have an interest in a family business would do well to discuss this early on in the application process and understand what limits, if any, may be placed on this continuing affiliation, should they be accepted. In some instances, their investment opportunities may be constrained as well. In general, most agents have no problem living with these restrictions, as there are thousands of investment and savings opportunities still open to them. They are also required to keep their personal finances in reasonable order. That is, they are expected to pay lawful debts, maintain reasonable credit, and the like. In rare instances an agent may have to file for bankruptcy. This could affect their ability to maintain a security clearance, and since all agents have top secret security clearances, this might affect their continued employment.

Some new agents come to the FBI out of the military and may still have or seek to retain a reserve obligation. Some do this because they do not want to sever their ties to the military; others because they want to maintain their military skills, such as being in flight status; and still others because they hope to qualify for a military pension. The FBI has struggled long and hard with these issues and has, over the years, adopted a policy that an agent cannot be a member of an active reserve unit. While the FBI understands the desire of some to continue to serve their country by maintaining their military affiliation, the demands of the FBI and the military can often clash. The events of 9/11 are a perfect example, when the FBI redirected massive numbers of agents to terrorism investigations at the same time as the military was calling up reserve units to deal with its increased operational needs. The individual who is an agent and an active reserve member simply cannot be in both places at once, thus the requirement that they must sever their reserve obligations.

The FBI as an Extended Family

Foreign vacations as an FBI agent can be an experience like none other. Law enforcement is an extended family in many ways. Agents planning a foreign trip will often make inquiries of friends as to law enforcement contacts in the foreign country. Since many law enforcement officials attend international conferences and meetings, it is customary for the host agency to extend numerous social privileges to their guests. These are reciprocated in kind when someone is visiting the recipient of such courtesies. A simple phone call to an unmet colleague in a foreign country will usually prompt offers of pick-ups at airports, departmental tours, and tips on hotels, restaurants, sightseeing, and much more. Often these occasions are the forum for the exchange of gifts as well, normally memorabilia and clothing from one's home agency.

Some agents choose to join the FBI Agents' Association (FBIAA) while on duty. This is an organization that functions to some small degree like a union, offering additional benefits to agents, like life insurance. The association also represents the agent workforce in dealings with FBI management on issues of discipline, employment, and related matters, and from time to time it will take public positions on issues in the criminal justice community. The FBI is exempt from unionization under the provisions of Title 7 of the Civil Service Reform Act of 1978, so the FBIAA is the closest thing to one most agents will ever see. The FBIAA in many cities is particularly active in sponsoring charity golf tournaments. These events are well attended by both active and retired agents and also support personnel, and are a good opportunity for people to stay in touch and have fun while supporting a good cause.

Another organization some agents choose to join is the Federal Law Enforcement Officers Association. The group is similar to FBIAA, but is composed primarily of federal investigators from other agencies. Other organizations also exist for law-enforcement officers, their membership based on gender or ethnic background.

Still other agents choose to join either the Fraternal Order of Police (FOP) or the Police Benevolent Association (PBA). Both are old, well-established organizations that primarily represent the interests of uniformed law-enforcement personnel. They provide social and professional services and benefits and, in some areas, function as unions representing their members in contract negotiations and personnel matters. Agents cannot benefit from these services, but in areas where these organizations allow federal agents to join, many do so for personal and social reasons. Both FOP and PBA lodges and halls typically offer food, drink, and entertainment at greatly reduced prices. There are also dances and other social functions.

Your Relationships with Outsiders

There is the issue of how agents handle their interactions with friends and neighbors. Some choose to keep the fact of their employment close to the vest, while others are quite open about it. For those who choose to limit self-disclosure, this is easiest with casual friends. Neighbors are another matter, for they will notice the somewhat odd work hours; usually the radio and red or blue light in the company car are dead giveaways. Most agents choose to take a middle ground, letting people close to them emotionally and physically know who they are, but being more guarded with casual acquaintances.

Many agents become unofficial mentors owing to their employment being known. For instance, many young people are interested in the FBI, and it is not uncommon for an agent to be approached by friends, relatives, neighbors, and others to offer guidance to a child, niece, or nephew. Almost all agents welcome these requests, for it is an opportunity to afford a young person some guidance about the FBI and, also, the work of many other law-enforcement agencies that may seem distant and mysterious to newcomers.

Another facet of an agent's existence is stuff. "Stuff" refers to the innumerable FBI memorabilia available through the FBIRA. Sooner or later during the year, agents will find themselves giving out baseball hats, tee-shirts, warm-up jackets, notebooks, golf balls, and various other items bearing the FBI seal or name. Most are good-natured about it, but it can get a little expensive sometimes.

Some Final Considerations

No discussion of the Special Agent position would be complete without mentioning the dark secret that permeates all of law enforcement, be it federal, state, or local: stress. Law enforcement can be a tough way to make a living. The hours are unusual and demanding. The work, which may seem glamorous from the outside, can be brutal in reality. A violent crime scene is not a pretty thing to see, much less spend six hours processing. Many criminals are vicious and dangerous psychopaths who often live in squalor. Victims are often wrenching to deal with. The judicial process can appear tilted in favor of the bad guys and can be excruciatingly slow. Family life and patterns can be upset by the receipt of a telephone call. Many times agents and others in law enforcement make a conscious effort to shield their families from the realities of what they do and what they have seen in the course of their work. This may work for the family, but it can exacerbate the stress the law-enforcement professional already feels. Oftentimes, there is the perception that only those "on the job" really understand what the agent, detective, or officer is going through. One can get to the point of feeling in the world but at the same time being cut off from it.

For many years such issues were accepted as the cost of doing business and there was an unspoken belief that "tough cops don't let it get to them." Alcohol and reckless behavior were often seen as ways to blow off steam. Thankfully, beginning in the 1970s, such views began to change. The FBI and many other law-enforcement agencies began to study more closely the toll police work was taking on their members. Solutions such as the FBI's Employee Assistance Program were introduced and supervisory personnel were trained to spot and deal with early signs of psychological deterioration. The FBI and most police departments have close and active affiliations with various religious groups and support agencies that have chaplains and counselors available on demand. Most important, the unspoken, unwritten mantra that "real" cops and agents do not have problems was recognized as deeply flawed.

While much progress has been made, there is still a long way to go. Some studies indicate that 75 percent of all law-enforcement personnel will go through a divorce (the national average for all groups is about 50 percent). The Law Enforcement Wellness Association estimates that the rate of police suicides is three times the national average. The National Police Suicide Foundation believes police suicides are greatly underreported, and suspects that the suicide rate in law enforcement is more like five times the national average of about 12 suicides per 100,000 persons in the population. The foundation also believes this rate is even higher for retired or disabled officers.

Though such issues are painful to recount, they are a realistic consideration for one contemplating a career in law enforcement. Even allowing for the demands of the job, lest you think that employment as an FBI agent is akin to joining a cloistered religious order, it is not. Most agents live quite openly, and many are involved in civic activities as coaches, volunteers for various causes, Scout leaders, local (unpaid) councilpersons, religious leaders, and more. Most achieve a balance between the demands of the job and responsibilities to their families and communities. Owing to the high esteem most persons have for the FBI, agents are often sought out by their fellow citizens to assume roles involving leadership and responsibility. In short, most make it work and have both challenging FBI careers and full and rewarding family and personal lives, although there can be a few rough spots along the way. In reality, these demands are probably not appreciably greater than those involved in many positions in the military or corporate America.

Agents also have political views, just like their fellow citizens. Their participation in the American politic process is not constrained in any way, with two caveats. They cannot, as an FBI agent, make their participation seem like it represents the Bureau's position, and because of federal laws on the subject, they cannot use government time, money, facilities, or resources to advance their political agenda.

Service as an FBI Agent is a full, rewarding, challenging, intriguing, and productive career. Most persons do it successfully and a few brilliantly. It is, however, not for everyone, and the wise applicant would do well to consider its many ramifications before deciding to proceed further.

Career Paths

The vast majority of FBI agents begin and end their careers as street agents, conducting investigations. For almost all that time, this is a full and satisfying career. They spend their days working cases, running surveillances, reviewing documents, collecting evidence, participating in training, conducting interviews, preparing reports, testifying, and making arrests.

Most agents will probably have served in two or three field offices and perhaps been assigned to one or two "Specials" along the way. A Special is a task force type of investigation involving a high-profile matter, such as the explosion of TWA Flight 800 over Long Island Sound or the 1996 bombing at Olympic Park in Atlanta. Agents may also have developed specialized skills to perform collateral duties in addition to their investigative assignments. These could include serving as firearms instructor; language speaker; Evidence Response Team member; SWAT team member; hostage negotiator; police instructor; pilot; polygraph examiner; technical agent (one who installs court-authorized wiretaps); informant coordinator; canine search specialist; or applicant recruiter. In larger offices where the workload demands are greater, these positions may be full-time jobs.

This chapter reviews both the regular career paths and some alternative choices that are available to those who achieve success in the Bureau. Let's begin by looking at some of the ways a street agent might come to consider a change in career path, then look at the more usual routes agents follow up the ladder.

It is appropriate, also, at this point to bring up the often contentious issue of politics. It simply does not exist in the FBI. With the exception of the director, who may be appointed partially on the basis of his or her political affiliation, there is no consideration of politics in FBI appointments or promotions. All FBI promotions are made based on the recommendation of career boards. These are standing bodies of more senior FBI personnel who review the qualifications of each applicant and vigorously debate their relative merits.

Career boards can be lengthy and excruciating exercises for the participants, since each candidate is personally interviewed to allow the individual to make his or her own case for promotion. With multiple candidates for popular or career-enhancing promotions, a career board may have to sit for a day or more to evaluate all who have applied.

Career Directions Frequently Change

Sometimes, getting involved in particular duties causes an agent to reassess his or her career plans. An agent who teaches at a lot of police schools may decide that he would like to perform these duties full time, and will begin to orient his career toward an assignment at the Training Academy at Quantico. Another agent who is a part-time pilot may seek a transfer to a larger office where she would be able to fly full time. A SWAT team member who splits his time between performing normal investigative duties and training for SWAT operations may decide to apply for the Hostage Rescue Team (HRT). HRT, stationed at Quantico, is a sort of "super-SWAT" team that is deployed in only the most high-risk, sensitive operations. HRT members have no investigative assignments, and they train on a full-time basis.

Many HRT members go through U.S. Army Ranger or U.S. Navy Seal training in preparation for their duties.

Some of the larger FBI offices have units called Special Operations Groups (SOG). These are composed of experienced agents who are assigned primarily surveillance duties on a full-time basis. They do not differ in grade from their counterparts in the field office and in larger facilities, called "off-sites," they have an on-scene supervisory special agent. They operate from covert locations and drive a mixture of private and commercial vehicles. Many alter their dress and personal appearance to more closely blend into the civilian population of the area. Their work is usually in support of another agent's case and may assist in helping map the organization and membership of a criminal enterprise; observe criminal acts in real time, such as a dope deal or bribe payment; or help develop evidence to support an application for a search warrant or wiretap, referred to in the FBI as a Title III, from the section of the criminal code where such activities are authorized. Agents on such squads are skilled in the use of cameras and video surveillance equipment.

Service as an SOG agent can be a bit of an adventure at times. FBI agents are expected to obey all laws, including speed limits and stop signs, unless responding to a crime with light and siren operating. Maintaining contact with a surveillance subject can present challenges, and creativity is at a premium. (In FBI investigations, all persons who are the subject of an investigation are called, logically, "subjects." If in an investigation the name of the subject is not known, the person is referred to as "unknown subject" or "unsub.") Disruptions can also occur. An agent could be following the same person for days or weeks and the person's routine never varies. The suspect might drive in his neighborhood for several hours, maintaining an apparently normal pattern. Then, one day, he might get into his vehicle as usual and drive a thousand miles overnight to a location he has never gone to before. The surveillance cannot be broken and, while the SOG agent can request assistance from FBI field office territories he is passing through, the agent may wind up spending the night many miles from home. Accordingly, most SOG agents have a couple of changes of clothes and some toilet articles in the trunks of their vehicles. When away from home on operational issues, SOG and indeed all agents are permitted reasonable use of FBI telephones to maintain contact with their families. They are also entitled to housing and meal allowances when in such a status.

Large FBI field offices may also have another entity, called a Special Support Group (SSG). These function much in the manner of the SOGs with one important exception. SSGs are staffed with nonagent personnel, who are not armed. SSG units are used on less sensitive and less dangerous surveillances. Service on an SSG is about as close as one can come to the duties of an agent without actually becoming one. (It is also noted that under current FBI policy, SSG service can give one some degree of preference when applying for the Special Agent position.)

The Agency Hot List

The Personal Resource List (PRL) is something many agents watch more closely than their bank accounts. This is the mechanism many use for making a career change. Here's how it works. Every field office has a target staffing level for both agent and nonagent personnel. When the agent complement of an office falls below this level owing to resignation, retirement, promotion, or transfer, the Special Agent Transfer Unit looks to the PRL for replacements. The PRL is maintained for each office and agents on that list are in order by seniority of Bureau service. Thus, someone on the PRL for Phoenix who began duty as an agent on March 15, 1999, would be higher up on that list than anyone who became an agent after that date, but lower than anyone who started earlier.

Each agent is allowed to pick one PRL office and is, in essence, saying, "If there is ever an opening, I would like to go." Several times a year an agent may change his or her PRLP (Personal Resource List Program) designation, and some agents actively "shop" these lists among several offices in which they have an interest, looking one on which their seniority places them in a more competitive position. The government pays for these transfers, since the FBI needs to fill office vacancies as they occur. An agent is entitled to one PRL transfer in his or her career.

Often, agents within a few years of retirement will seek a PRL transfer to the area where they hope to retire. Accordingly, the competition for popular retirement regions is intense. Becoming involved in the Career Development Program (CDP) will, for all practical purposes, take an agent out of the PRL process, since work location is determined by the demands of that program. An agent who chooses to leave the CDP can later reenter the PRL process, however.

Usually, the only exception to having seniority on a PRL is having a specialty. For example, if a field office lost a Russian speaker to retirement, the most senior Russian speaker on the PRL for that office would be offered the transfer. The Russian speaker would jump over more senior agents who did not have the specialty. This is one reason many agents try to develop a collateral specialty, such as being a firearms instructor, pilot, or hostage negotiator.

There is also a special category of interoffice change called a hardship transfer. These are compassionate transfers made, at Bureau expense, to accommodate a serious family problem, almost always medically related and involving a spouse, parent, or child. Hardships, as they are called in the Bureau, are relatively rare.

Street Agent

The life of a street agent is one of considerable freedom, within the bounds of being assigned to a squad in a field office and having a Supervisory Special Agent as boss. Older, experienced agents are given wide latitude to pursue their cases pretty much as they see fit, within the bounds of FBI policy and the law. They may come into the office but once or twice a week, and with access to a Bureau vehicle, modern communications systems, and improving computer networks and equipment, they can run and coordinate fairly complex investigations.

The combination of challenging and interesting work, the satisfaction of making a difference in the service of one's country, being afforded respect and standing in one's community, the opportunity to develop a specialty skill in an area you find interesting, competitive pay and benefits, relative freedom, a government vehicle, good companionship in the FBI and the larger law-enforcement community, productive relationships with local law-enforcement agencies, an adequate retirement plan, and the possibility of a PRL transfer someday make being a street agent as far as many want to go. As one old-time agent is reported to have once said, "Where else can you make this much money asking questions?"

One of the major advantages to being a street agent is the incredible variety of experiences the job affords. An agent may work an organized crime surveillance one week, be assigned to monitor a wiretap the next, be involved in planning and executing a fugitive arrest the next week, and end the month in a distant city conducting a police school for state and local law-enforcement officers.

So, too, an agent's exposure to people of varied backgrounds can be rewarding. The FBI is mainly a collector of information, and most information comes from people. The ability to conduct interviews is one of the most prized and useful skills an FBI agent can possess, for an astonishing variety of people will be participants in those interviews. In the course of one week one may interview a local pastor, a felon with multiple convictions, a scared witness to a crime, a potential informant who may have a severe drug problem, and the former girlfriend of a fugitive. One must be able to deal with a wide variety of people, understand their needs and motivations, assess the accuracy and completeness of what they are speaking about, and use a combination of learned skills and intuition to fully develop whatever information they may have of value. Oftentimes, it is desirable to develop the basis of a long-term relationship with these people, as well. The witnesses with useful information may not testify for a year or more, if ever, but their confidence in the interviewing agent must remain strong, if they are needed. Likewise, the informant may be a continuing source of information on criminal activities for months or even years. The fugitive's ex-girlfriend may know nothing of value at this point, but may learn something of value a month from now.

Long-term relationships with "straight" people are also important and exciting, be they professionals, businesspeople, or others. Many times someone will bring information to an agent basically because they have known them a long time and trust them. A prominent businessperson will probably not report a dope deal, for it is unlikely he will have information about such activities. But the individual could well report a corrupt politician he has heard of or had dealings with. Information sources can vary widely, but all are useful and make the work interesting.

On the other hand, some street agents decide to pursue what is called administrative advancement, or further career development. The normal first step is to volunteer for and be appointed to a relief supervisor position on the squad to which they are assigned. The agent will receive a modest amount of training, but will mainly learn on the job as he or she fills in for the boss several days a month. This allows the agent to begin to learn the boss's job by reviewing reports and communications written by other agents, assigning cases, planning raids and arrests, and performing a variety of administrative duties. After a suitable period as a relief supervisor, an agent can then begin to apply for Supervisory Special Agent positions in that field office, another field office, or FBI Headquarters.

Field Supervisor (Supervisory Special Agent)

For agents selected to be Field Supervisors, many will choose to end their careers in these positions. In many ways they parallel the benefits of being a street agent, with a little more pay and influence thrown in. This is particularly true for Field Supervisors who happen to like the office and area to which they are assigned. The ability to do this has, however, been the subject of vigorous policy debates within the FBI for many years. FBI Headquarters has, from time to time, instituted a policy that a Field Supervisor must transfer to FBI Headquarters after five years of service or step down to a street agent position. Such agents are not subject to transfer, but merely return to investigative duties in their field office. The essential duty of a Field Supervisor is to run a squad.

Headquarters Supervisor

Other agents, after several years as Field Supervisors, begin to apply for Headquarters Supervisor positions. There is no difference in pay or rank in moving from the field to Headquarters, but Headquarters experience is crucial if an agent is to have any chance of moving beyond the supervisor role. Headquarters Supervisors have largely administrative jobs in one of FBI Headquarters' divisions. Some positions, such as the Office of General Counsel or the Laboratory Division, may require special educational or professional qualifications, but most Headquarters assignments require only a solid investigative and administrative background.

Headquarters Supervisors are often the main point of contact between FBI Headquarters and the field offices. All criminal, intelligence, and terrorism violations investigated by the FBI are grouped into programs. Thus, an agent assigned to FBI Headquarters as a Headquarters Supervisor might, for example, be assigned to the Organized Crime (OC) section in the Criminal Investigative Division. Each violation relating to organized crime—racketeer-influenced corrupt organization, extortionate credit transactions (loan sharking), and the like—is grouped under the organized crime program. Each violation in that program has specified reporting requirements. Thus, the case agent in charge of an organized crime investigation in the field will have to prepare periodic reports to FBI Headquarters as to the progress being made in that case. A good bit of the role of the Headquarters Supervisor is to read these reports, summarize them for higher officials, and prepare communications going back to the field as to observations and next steps. Depending on the scope and import of such communications, they may require the approval of the supervisor's unit chief or much higher levels at Headquarters. Truly sweeping or critical communications may require the approval of the director.

Inspector's Aide

After several years as a Headquarters Supervisor, an agent can then apply for a position as an Inspector's Aide on the FBI Inspection Staff. This group performs operational and compliance inspections of all FBI field offices and Headquarters divisions about every two years. With over 50 field offices and about a dozen Headquarters divisions, the Inspection Staff is a busy place. A normal tour is one year, and Inspector's Aides can expect to be on the road three weeks a month. Family conflicts are always a concern for agents assigned to the Inspection Staff, but these, too, are good training for the future since further FBI career development will usually entail more moves and additional family disruption. For some, this is the end of the road from a career development viewpoint, since they realize the family costs are simply too high. Many of these agents will return to Headquarters or field supervisory assignments and finish their careers there, perhaps not having advanced as high as they might like but enjoying much more family harmony.

Those who are selected to serve on the Inspection Staff as Inspector's Aides will work in ad hoc teams that change from inspection to inspection. A team of aides works under the direction of one or more inspectors assigned to conduct a given inspection. During the course of an inspection of a field office, which may last from two to four weeks depending on the size of the office, an aide may help evaluate the office's compliance with financial management directives, the effectiveness of its organized crime program, and the condition of the office vehicle fleet. Other areas that fall within the purview of the inspection could include all investigative and administrative programs; informant operations; aviation operations; the training program; and scores of other matters.

It is difficult for an outsider to appreciate the scope and scale of an FBI inspection. Not only are the office and its operations inspected but the pulse of the community is taken. Interviews are conducted with prosecutors, judges, law-enforcement officials, the media, minority leaders, and others to gain a sense as to how the FBI is perceived in the area and whether it is addressing important crime, intelligence, or terrorism threats. Such findings are then incorporated into the overall inspection results.

Under the tenure of Director Louis Freeh, yet another Inspection Staff innovation was unveiled. This was an anonymous survey of the agent population in the office as to the effectiveness of the Special Agent in Charge (SAC) and other executives. Needless to say, this procedure was widely popular with the street agents and widely unpopular with many SACs.

Inspection Staff experience is viewed as critical to future career development for a number of reasons. First, there is the hands-on experience of dealing with and analyzing field office operations and programs. Second, there is the opportunity to see first-hand the management styles and problems of senior field executives. Third, there is the camaraderie developed with one's peers from around the country on the Inspection Staff, many of whom will advance to more senior positions in the FBI. Fourth, is the opportunity to work for various inspectors who are on the verge of assuming higher command positions within the FBI. Finally, there is the need to make tough, often confrontational decisions. Not all inspections go well, and it is not uncommon to prepare reports and findings that will not reflect well on a given field office or its senior management. Such reports can literally be career ending for the executives involved. The ability to discover, fully document, and present such findings and defend them in often emotional face-to-face meetings is considered an indicator of how an Inspector's Aide is likely to perform in more senior positions the person may hold later in his or her career. In FBI slang, the preparation and defense of critical findings and reports is referred to as "calling the hard shot." It is a process that is not always pretty, but it is considered vital to the continued health and effectiveness of the FBI as an organization.

Following service on the Inspection Staff, agents may return to their previous jobs or rotate to other Headquarters' Supervisor positions. At this point, the agent may choose to remain in a supervisory position at Headquarters for the remainder of his or her career. Others will try to advance at Headquarters by seeking, in order, positions as Unit Chief, Assistant Section Chief, Section Chief, Deputy Assistant Director, and Assistant Director. At each stage the agent will be accepting increasing levels of responsibility for the direction of a Headquarters investigative or administrative program. While some agents never again leave Headquarters as they move up the management ranks, the more common route to senior management positions is to alternate between increasingly responsible field and Headquarters assignments.

Assistant Special Agent in Charge

To achieve their career ends, following Inspection Staff service, many agents begin to apply for Assistant Special Agent in Charge (ASAC) positions. Competition for these positions can be especially keen, since the ASAC position is a gateway job considered essential to further career development. Accordingly, many people may apply for an ASAC opening, especially if it is in a highly desirable office. Other, less attractive, offices may attract only a handful of candidates.

The ASAC position is both a bottleneck and a platform for further career development. Many agents, after applying for many ASAC openings without success, resign themselves to finishing their careers in Headquarters' assignments. For those who succeed in gaining an ASAC position, one of the more exciting and informative stages of their career is about to begin. As the name implies, an ASAC is the number-two person in all but the very largest FBI field offices, which may have a number of ASACs under a Special Agent in Charge (SAC). The largest offices, such as New York City and Los Angeles, may have more than one SAC under the direction of an Assistant Director in Charge (ADIC).

ASACs deal with the full range of office operations and responsibilities. They are responsible for managing a number of investigative programs, overseeing the office's administrative operations, dealing with state and local law-enforcement officials, meeting with the public, resolving personnel issues, preparing budgets, working with federal prosecutors, representing the office at public events and inter-agency meetings, and filling in for the SAC when he or she is absent from the office.

The relationship between an SAC and ASAC can range from the formal to the friendly, but most are on the latter end of the spectrum. An SAC depends heavily on the ASAC and has often had dealings with the individual earlier. Oftentimes, an SAC will act as a mentor to the ASAC throughout the remainder of their respective careers in the FBI. There is an old joke in the FBI that each SAC has, somewhere in the confines of his or her desk, a large "ASAC Handle" stamp that's used whenever the SAC gets an onerous or tedious assignment. There is some truth in this, in that ASACs must learn the full range of a SAC's duties, which can certainly include administrative matters that are not much fun. By and large, SACs are quite fair in seeing to it that their ACASs see enough of the fun stuff also to balance out the work load.

There is a phenomenon in the FBI that is common to many organizations. As noted, someone in the Career Development Program (CDP) may work for an inspector or SAC and develop a mentor–mentoree relationship with the individual. This can be a powerful asset as the more senior person rises through the Bureau's ranks. For many years in the FBI this was referred to as a "guy" thing. Let us say there was a high Bureau official with the nickname "Duke," who watched out for three or four younger FBI executives as they made their way up the FBI hierarchy. The word would quickly spread that so-and-so was a "Duke guy," meaning that Duke was his unofficial patron and sponsor. This is well and good, and part of human nature, until Duke retires or falls out of favor. The patron is either gone or diminished, but the label remains and may come back to haunt one in a political sense.

Following several years' successful service as an ASAC, an agent may begin to apply for positions at Headquarters, such as Section Chief or Inspector. In rare instances, an ASAC may rise directly to an SAC position either in the same office or in another FBI office.

Headquarters Section Chief or Inspector

As a Section Chief at Headquarters, an agent is responsible for running an FBI investigative or administrative program. These programs could range from organized crime investigations to space management, from FBI purchasing operations to Cuban counterintelligence investigations, or from personnel management operations to public and congressional relations. These are positions of considerable scope and responsibility. Section Chiefs are the equivalent of Major General (two-star) positions in the military. Persons at or above the level of Section Chief or Special Agent in Charge are made members of the Senior Executive Service (SES), which spans the federal government. Almost none will ever leave the FBI, but technically the individual could move to another federal agency, since the creation of the SES was meant to facilitate inter-agency movement of key executives.

Inspectors, as noted in the discussion of the operations of the FBI Inspector's Aide, lead inspections of FBI field offices, Legal Attaché offices, and Headquarters divisions. On occasion they are detailed to lead major "specials," which are task force investigations into major, high-profile incidents or crimes.

Special Agent in Charge

Those entering the SAC position will normally have been Inspectors or Section Chiefs. Upon assuming the SAC position, they become the

FBI's representatives within their field office territories, with full responsibility for all FBI operations and programs. Many see the SAC position as the culmination of a successful career and are more than happy to serve out the rest of their careers there. A SAC is one of the top federal officials in their area of operations, and depending on the population density of the area, may be responsible for an entire state or group of states. Accordingly, they deal often with Governors and other top state officials, U.S. Senators and Representatives, ranking federal officials, the business and professional communities, and frequently the media. They are often in the public eye and, in that state, are the living embodiment of the FBI. While SACs occupy an exalted position in the FBI hierarchy, they are still Special Agents and must comply with all the requirements of that position. They must be physically fit, maintain a desirable weight, and qualify with firearms four times a year.

There is no set or required way for a SAC to run the field office, and that is one of the attractions of the job. The individual can run it in any manner he or she sees fit, provided the SAC obeys FBI policies, is fair, and has an effective and efficient operation. Some SACs are detail-oriented taskmasters while others are big-picture people. Some are somewhat aloof and require that things work their way up to them through the field-office chain of command, while others are often in the trenches with the troops. A few SACs prefer to remain largely in the area of their office (called "headquarters city" in the FBI) while others prefer to visit all their resident agencies (RAs) on a regular basis. They may do this by driving, using public transportation, or using Bureau aircraft. Almost every FBI field office has one or more aircraft assigned to it, and if it is not being used on an operational matter, the SAC may use it, consistent with Bureau policy.

If there is a line-of-duty law-enforcement death in the SAC's territory, the SAC is expected to attend as the FBI's official representative. Some SACs also take their supervisory staff with them to such events. SACs also are often invited to be present at, or even speak to, graduation classes from state and local law-enforcement agencies. They sometimes attend luncheons of the local chapters of the Society of Former Special Agents of the FBI and may also participate in social events and golf outings of the FBI National Academy Associates. They host visiting law-enforcement dignitaries, be they U.S. or foreign, and these events often involve their spouse. Trips to Washington, D.C., are frequent, as there are always matters that require consultation. And once every year or so, they and their spouse attend the Special Agents in Charge conference, which brings all SACs together for the better part of a week with ranking officials from FBI Headquarters for policy discussions and social events.

Some SACs have been unusually adept and innovative in involving the local communities they serve with the FBI, through citizens outreach programs and other activities. In some FBI field offices, SACs have pioneered "CEO Days" to acquaint local business and community leaders with the FBI and its mission. These events often involve bringing these guests to the FBI firearms range, where they are fitted with an official FBI baseball hat and allowed to fire the full range of FBI weapons, under the watchful eyes of FBI firearms instructors. Even the most hardened business executives can revert to 10 years old when allowed to "play" with "neat" guns. Such contacts can be invaluable to the FBI in many ways.

For example, if a local real estate developer has been to a CEO Day, and if the FBI needs a fixed surveillance location in the future, much can be accomplished in a short period of time. (A fixed surveillance location is just that—an apartment, store, or house from which another fixed location can be easily observed.) A simple call to a CEO "friend" can expedite the provision of an apartment on very short notice and with a minimum of fuss and paperwork. The Bureau is able to pay for such facilities, but getting them quickly and quietly can make or break the success of an investigation.

Other SACs have developed Citizen's Academies in their field offices. These are similar in many ways to the CEO Days, but are open to a larger and broader cross-section of the community. The first Citizen's Academy was started in 1993, and since then over 5,000 people have gone through them. The program generally lasts about 10 weeks and is attended by local officials and people from the business and private sectors. The participants attend lectures and demonstrations on terrorism, securities fraud, organized crime, counterintelligence, and fugitive apprehension. At the end, participants may be able to fire the range of weapons used by the FBI in its work. Most citizens enjoy the experience immensely and leave with a better understanding of the FBI and its mission, and also an appreciation that FBI people are people like themselves.

The SACs represent the FBI on the Federal Executive Board (FEB) in their city or region. The FEB comprises the heads of various federal agencies located in the area, be they civilian or military. The role of the FEB is to address various issues of interest to the federal government in that locale. Such issues could include pay rates; recruiting; on-street parking allocations for federal vehicles; relationships with the General Services Administration (GSA), which is the landlord for all federal office buildings; relationships with various state and local agencies; or the Combined Federal campaign (CFC). The CFC is the yearly charitable solicitation of all federal employees, much like the United Way in the private sector. Employees wishing to contribute can do so through payroll deductions and, further, can direct their contributions to charities of their choice. A federal employee cannot be penalized in any way for electing not to participate in the CFC.

For these and many other reasons, the SAC position is often called "the best job in the Bureau." An agent selected to be a SAC normally starts in a smaller FBI field office, with 50 to 100 Special Agents assigned. After several years of successful service as an SAC, an agent may be considered for assignment as an SAC in a larger FBI field office. Some SACs desire and pursue such opportunities while others vigorously resist them, since they are content in their existing assignments. Still other first-time SACs pursue or accept reassignment back to Headquarters as Deputy Assistant Directors (DAD) or Assistant Directors in Charge of a Headquarters division. In general terms, a

DAD serves an ADIC at Headquarters in much the same manner as an ASAC serves a SAC in a field office—as a principal deputy.

Interesting Alternatives

In the midst of the vertical progression that consumes the majority of FBI executive careers, there are a number of interesting sidebars. These are both irrelevant and important to the career progression of those destined for higher positions in the Bureau. They are relevant, since they are awarded to those deemed likely to assume higher positions in the FBI. They are irrelevant in that they are, while important, well outside the traditional forms of FBI career development.

Executive Training Programs

For many years, the FBI has welcomed law-enforcement and intelligence professionals from outside the Bureau into its training and career development programs on a limited basis. Likewise, many outside entities have offered the FBI slots in some of their most prestigious training programs. Thus, do FBI agents on the career track to even higher positions in the FBI take time out to attend some of the most coveted and sought-after executive training programs in the world. These include, among others, the Senior Executive Officers Course at the Australian Police Staff College; the Program for Senior Managers in Government at the Kennedy School of Government at Harvard University; the National Executive Institute; the senior development program at the Army War College at Carlisle Barracks, Carlisle, Pennsylvania; a similar senior course at the Naval War College, Newport, Rhode Island; and the United Kingdom's leading course for future law-enforcement executives at the police academy at Bramshill, England.

Generally, these courses last from three or four weeks to several months. Some may last an entire year. They are exciting, enriching, career enhancing, and broadening. They also prepare the FBI attendee for future FBI service from a more worldly perspective. They are also fun, as someone who has spent the majority of his or her adult life in the FBI is exposed to other ambitious, talented people from very different walks of life.

Leaving the FBI

There is yet another avenue that departs from the normal FBI career path: leaving the FBI. While not common, there have been instances in which mid-career and even senior FBI executives have made lateral transitions to other federal agencies. This is especially easy for those in the Senior Executive Service, which was developed to promote inter-agency movement of executives. Some agents in the past left to become part of the Inspector General's Office of the U.S. Department of Labor, while another became the Inspector General of the Department of Agriculture, a position that required Senate confirmation.

Other Career Paths

While the discussion thus far has described the majority of the FBI career development system, there are three other major categories of career choices available to agents: Resident Agency, Legal Attaché, and Quantico.

Senior and Supervisory Senior Resident Agents

Resident agencies (RAs) are as old as the FBI itself. They are suboffices out of a major (headquarters city) office. Thus, for example, the Miami field office has RAs in West Palm Beach, Homestead, Fort Pierce, and Key West. An RA may have only a single agent assigned or as many as 40 or 50, and may be responsible for only one county or half a state. In every RA there is a Senior Resident Agent. This person performs semi-supervisory duties in smaller RAs of fewer than eight agents. Larger RAs will have a Supervisory Senior Resident Agent (SSRA) who gets supervisory pay and is considered part of the regular FBI career development system. SSRAs are equivalent to field supervisors in a field office. Very large RAs—say, of 30 or more agents—may be headed by an ASAC. Special Agents assigned to an RA are themselves referred to as RAs (Resident Agents).

Being an RA is considered by many agents to be an ideal assignment for a number of reasons. Usually, the level of supervision is looser than at the headquarters city, giving agents more leeway in how they pursue their assignments. Second, living costs are usually lower and commuting is easier. Third, family life is often richer and less hectic. Fourth, there is a closer relationship to the community and to local law-enforcement agencies and officials. Fifth, federal pay scales often make RAs among the highest paid members of their communities. Sixth, in less urban areas there is even more prestige in being an FBI agent. Finally, since the RA is solely responsible for all FBI interests in the area, there is a greater variety of assignments and less specialization than at the headquarters city.

Legal Attaché

Legal Attachés (Legats, pronounced LEE-gats) have a long and rich history in the FBI, having been in existence for over 50 years. A Legat is an FBI office attached to a U.S. Embassy in a foreign country. They primarily perform liaison duties, coordinate international criminal and counterintelligence investigations, arrange training, assist foreign agencies with investigations with the United States, and represent the FBI's and sometimes the Department of Justice's interests in the area. Some Legats service only one country while others may cover a number of countries in their region.

While Legats have been in existence for some time, their number has soared in the past three decades, fueled by the need for better international coordination and cooperation in organized crime, drug cartel, and terrorism investigations. Also contributing to this growth was the demise of the former Soviet Union, which opened a number of former Cold War adversaries to opportunities for cooperation with U.S. law enforcement. Within the FBI, the term Legat refers both to a Legal Attaché office and to an agent assigned to one of them.

Legats come from a variety of backgrounds within the FBI, but all have a solid investigative background before receiving such a posting. Many come from counterintelligence backgrounds, as much Legat work involves espionage investigations. A Legat office certainly pays due deference to the ambassador in whose Embassy they reside, but they do not report to them. They are under the direction of FBI Headquarters, and contrary to what some movies might suggest, they rarely carry weapons or conduct actual investigations outside the United States. Legat agents typically carry supervisory or unit chief status, in recognition of the importance and sensitivity of their duties. As might be expected, foreign-language ability is usually desirable and in some instances mandatory. Legats' families usually accompany them and there are generous financial arrangements to provide for the maintenance of one's home residence in the United States while the agent is serving abroad in a Legat status. Also, as might be expected in a foreign liaison posting, there are significant entertainment demands. Most Legats complete one or two tours in the Legat system, then return to the mainstream FBI management positions. The average Legat tour overseas is four years.

At present, the FBI has 48 Legal Attaché offices and 6 Legat suboffices, located in the following areas:

Abu Dhabi, United Arab Emirates
Almaty, Kazakhstan
Amman, Jordan
Ankara, Turkey
Athens, Greece
Bangkok, Thailand
Beijing, China
Berlin, Germany
Bern, Switzerland
Bogota, Columbia
Brasilia, Brazil
Bridgetown, Barbados

Brussels, Belgium
Bucharest, Romania
Buenos Aires, Argentina
Cairo, Egypt
Canberra, Australia
Caracas, Venezuela
Copenhagen, Denmark
Frankfurt Suboffice, Germany
Guadalajara Suboffice, Mexico
Hermosillo Suboffice, Mexico
Hong Kong, China
Islamabad, Pakistan
Kiev, Ukraine
Kuala Lumpur, Malaysia
Lagos, Nigeria
London, England
Madrid, Spain
Manila, Philippines
Mexico City, Mexico
Monterray Suboffice, Mexico
Moscow, Russia
Nairobi, Kenya
New Delhi, India
Ottawa, Canada
Panama City, Panama
Paris, France
Prague, Czech Republic
Pretoria, South Africa
Rabat, Morocco
Riyadh, Saudi Arabia
Rome, Italy
Santiago, Chile
Santo Domingo, Dominican Republic
Seoul, South Korea

Singapore, Singapore
Tallinn, Estonia
Tel Aviv, Israel
Tokyo, Japan
Tuijuana Suboffice, Mexico
Vienna, Austria
Warsaw, Poland

The remaining two foreign locations to which agents are posted on a regular basis are the International Law Enforcement Academy, Budapest, Hungary; and INTERPOL, located in Lyon, France. INTERPOL was founded in 1923 and has 182 countries as members. Its overall objective is to optimize international law-enforcement efforts, and it focuses on three core services: providing a unique core law-enforcement communications system; providing a range of databases and analytic services; and providing proactive support for police services around the world.

As the above list of Legat locations indicates, some of these positions are in some volatile parts of the world. Not all Legat assignments are, thus, tea and cookies assignments. In some countries, Legats and their families live in guarded compounds and travel in armored vehicles with bodyguards. For those worried about such situations, they should note that all Legat assignments are voluntary.

At this point it is likely the Legat program will only grow larger. As the FBI gains experience in staffing and operating far-flung Legats, it is more open to requests from potential host countries for assistance.

Quantico

Quantico is a place, a division of FBI Headquarters, and a way of life. The FBI's Training Division is housed on the huge Marine Corps base at Quantico, Virginia, about 40 miles south of Washington, D.C. The FBI has trained FBI agents and other law-enforcement personnel there since the 1930s. The FBI Academy, as the complex is known, consists of 385 acres, three dormitories, a dining hall, library, four-story classroom building, 1,000-seat auditorium, the Forensic Science Research and Training Center, a chapel, an indoor firearms range, eight outdoor firearms ranges, four skeet ranges, a 200-yard rifle range, gun cleaning rooms and an armorer's shop, administrative offices, conference and meeting rooms, a 1.1-mile pursuit/defensive driving track, a gymnasium, an obstacle course, a pub, the Hogan's Alley practical problem mock city, a shooting house used in training by the Hostage Rescue Team, a store for basic needs and also law-enforcement memorabilia, a post office, and tennis courts and other recreational areas. The Academy, which is a secure facility not open to the pubic, is also the training location for the Drug Enforcement Administration.

Most of the training staff at Quantico are agents, many with advanced degrees. For a number of years the Academy has also had a strong academic relationship with the University of Virginia. Generally, agents assigned to the Academy have five to ten years' FBI experience and may well have been involved in training activities in their field offices. Some may have served as a counselor for the FBI National Academy, a quarterly 11-week training program run at the Academy for senior law-enforcement personnel from the United States and around the world. Others have served as counselors for New Agents Training classes.

FBI agents assigned to Quantico hold the rank of Headquarters Supervisors and are considered to be fully involved in the FBI career development programs. There are also unit chiefs, section chiefs, and higher ranks stationed at Quantico. Agents assigned to Quantico may teach a variety of law-enforcement topics, such as firearms, arrest techniques and planning, legal issues, collection of evidence, high-speed and pursuit driving, management, investigation of serial criminals, forensic accounting, and much more. Their students may be new agents, experienced agents returning for specialized or refresher training (called in-services), or U.S. and foreign police officers attending the FBI National Academy program. Agents assigned to Quantico are also involved in various research projects on law-enforcement matters. While Quantico agents may rotate back into the mainstream career development progression, a fair number decide to stay there for the remainder of their careers.

Other entities are also housed within the Quantico complex. These include the very elite Hostage Rescue Team, the profiling unit made famous in the movie *The Silence of the Lambs*, and a significant complex devoted to high-technology development of law enforcement tools and techniques.

Conclusion

The FBI is so large, complex, and dynamic an organization that, were this chapter twice as long, certain FBI Agent jobs would still be overlooked, since agents do an incredible variety of things: serve as liaison to the U.S. Olympic Committee; assist certain committees of Congress with inquiries; serve as the Chief of Police of Puerto Rico; sit on the Financial Action Task Force, the primary body in the United States for setting anti–money laundering policy; perform liaison duties at the White House; provide drug abuse and gambling awareness training to professional sports teams; mentor inner-city school kids; and provide counterintelligence and antiterrorism awareness training to U.S. businesses.

Recently it was reported that another agent, featured in national press stories, specializes in investigating the sale of phony sports memorabilia on the Internet. Another group of agents operates as the art crime team, maintaining a presence in the major art markets in the United States: New York, Los Angeles, Philadelphia, San Francisco, Indianapolis, St. Louis, and Salt Lake City. Their goal is to defeat trafficking in stolen works and sovereign cultural treasures estimated to be as high as $8 billion a year. Yet another agent was featured in a news article on the work he had been doing for the last ten years exposing fake war heroes (it is a federal offense to improperly wear a military uniform or decoration). The article went on to note that the number of persons now claiming to have been prisoners of war in Vietnam—about 1,000—exceeds the number who were actually released in 1973 (661). Some fakers commit their deeds for attention and glory while others carry out their charades to commit various forms of fraud. Recent press reports noted that the FBI has formed jewelry task forces in nine cities to team with state and local agencies to defeat well-organized ethnic gangs that routinely loot the jewelry industry, salespersons, and trade shows of millions of dollars each year.

One word of caution, however. While some of the above assignments sound pretty neat, hardly any of them are filled with new agents. Such assignments are usually given to agents who have five to ten years' experience and have earned the respect of their peers and superiors. There is no stronger recommendation in the FBI than a solid investigative track record. Once an agent has that, he or she can request and will often receive some of the more exciting and interesting assignments.

The Application Process

Note: FBI hiring policies and procedures are constantly evolving. While this chapter is accurate at the time it is written, you would be well served to inquire of your local FBI field office for any changes that may have been made.

It is easiest to think of the Special Agent application process as requiring you to pass through two gates. Successfully passing through the first gate requires meeting one of the *minimum qualifications* for the position of Special Agent. At present, these are:

- Having a Juris Doctor degree from a recognized university
- Being a certified public accountant (CPA)
- Having a resident four-year degree from a recognized college or university and having substantial language ability in a critical language
- Having a computer science degree or one of two recognized computer certifications
- Having a resident four-year degree from a recognized college or university and having three years' responsible work experience,

or having a graduate degree and two years' responsible work experience

If you meet one or more of the minimum requirements, passing through the second gate requires that your abilities fall into one of the FBI's *critical skills* categories. Although its needs have changed from time to time, the FBI routinely places applicants into several critical skills categories. Each year it attempts to hire a certain number of people from each category. Thus, if the FBI has 900 Special Agent slots to fill in a given year, a certain percentage of new openings will come from each category. Obviously, some categories have more applicants than others, making the competition for available positions in those categories more intense. As of 2005, the categories the Bureau is using are:

• *Engineering.* Candidates must have a degree in an engineering-related discipline. Degrees in architecture also suffice. Electrical engineers may be able to qualify under an expedited entry program that does not require three years' work experience.

• *Physical Science.* Candidates must have a degree in a scientific field such as physics, chemistry, nursing, biology, forensics, medical specialties, biochemistry, or mathematics.

• *Accounting/Financial.* Candidates must qualify under either the Accounting Special Entry Program (ASEP) or another program category and have a degree in accounting, finance, or a related field. To qualify under ASEP, the candidate must essentially be a certified pubic accountant (CPA).

• *Law/Law Enforcement/Military.* Candidates must qualify under the law program and have a JD degree from a U.S. law school. Law enforcement candidates must have at least two years' full-time investigative experience in a law-enforcement agency. Military candidates must have at least two years' full-time experience in the military.

• *Language.* Candidates may qualify if they have either a BS or a BA degree. They may pass both the listening and reading portions of the Defense Language Proficiency Test (DLPT) and achieve a score of 3 or higher on the Speaking Proficiency Test (SPT) in a critical language area. They may also be accepted by qualifying in another FBI hiring category and achieving a proficiency of 2+ in the SPT in a critical language area. In 2005, the critical languages were Arabic, Farsi, Pashtu, Urdu, Chinese (all dialects), Japanese, Korean, Russian, Spanish, and Vietnamese.

• *Intelligence (Military and Civilian).* Candidates must have at least two years' full-time experience in an intelligence activity. Time spent in intelligence training may also count toward this two-year requirement. For those already in an FBI support position, time spent as an Intelligence Analyst/Specialist or Special Surveillance Group member will suffice. This hiring category is being expanded to include persons with undergraduate or graduate degrees in international studies, international finance, or closely related programs.

• *Computer Science/Information Technology.* Candidates must have computer- or information technology–related degrees, a degree in electrical engineering, or be certified as a Cisco Certified Networking Professional (CCNP) or have a Cisco Certified Internet Expert (CCIE) certification.

Hiring Considerations

In many ways, the application process begins about a year earlier, in a meeting of assistant directors at FBI Headquarters. Once each year, these senior executives meet to decide the recruiting strategy of the FBI for the following year. Armed with substantial input from field offices and Headquarters divisions, as well as policy mandates from the Department of Justice, Office of Management and Budget, and congressional committees, this group fine-tunes the recruiting goals for Special Agents. Perhaps recent events have indicated a need for more accountants to handle corporate fraud investigations. If so, that category will be increased in the recruiting mix, usually with the result that another category's share of the applicant pool will decrease. The total number of agents hired in a given year is, obviously, set by Congress in the budget authority it provides the Bureau annually.

Over the years, the tendency of the FBI has been toward more specialization in its applicant goals. In years past, the number of agents coming out of the diversified programs was much greater and provided the FBI with persons experienced in a broad rage of professional fields. The FBI still seeks that mixture of backgrounds, but the demands brought about by 9/11 and various mandates placed on the FBI have generally directed recruiting efforts into more specialized channels.

While the FBI does not set specific targets for minorities and women, it has greatly improved its recruiting and hiring of both groups. The Bureau often participates in career days that target members of such groups and frequently visits colleges and universities with substantial minority or female populations. The Bureau is also active with professional groups that are based on specific interests, such as those representing minority attorneys and accountants.

Further Qualifications and Requirements

When individuals are interested in the FBI Special Agent position, they are directed to an FBI website where they are asked to fill out a short questionnaire. The purpose of these questions is to determine basic eligibility, such as being a U.S. citizen or a native of the Northern Mariana Islands; being over 23 years of age but not yet 37 at the time the application process will be completed; being available for assignment anywhere in the FBI's geographic jurisdiction; having no felony or major misdemeanor convictions; possessing a valid driver's license; and possessing at least a four-year degree from an accredited U.S. college or university. Since 9/11, this form also asks if the applicant falls into one of the critical skill categories noted above. Only those who do will proceed to the next stage of the process. This decision is made by a field office review board.

The age restriction is permitted by Public Law 93-50, which was passed on July 12, 1974, and allows the head of a federal agency to set maximum entry-on-duty ages for law-enforcement personnel, if done with the consent of the Office of Personnel Management. Owing to this age restriction, applicants are advised that it does not make much sense to apply if they are more than 36½ years old. This is because of the long time required to complete the application and then administer the tests and conduct the field background investigation.

Based on the information in the questionnaire, the application will be routed to the FBI field office that covers the applicant's area. This is normally one of three locations: the area in which the applicant lives, the area in which the individual works, or the area in which he or she is attending school. In the case of an applicant coming out of the military, determining location may be a bit more complex, as the individual may be deployed abroad or onboard ship.

As indicated in the questionnaire, there are a number of factors that automatically disqualify an applicant, among them conviction of a felony, default on a student loan insured by the U.S. government, failure on a drug test, or failure to register with the Selective Service System. Use of illegal drugs is also a disqualifier, under the following conditions:

- Use of marijuana within the past three years
- Use of marijuana more than 15 times in your life
- Use of any other illegal drug, including anabolic steroids after February 27, 1991, in the past 10 years
- Use of any other illegal drug, including anabolic steroids after February 27, 1991, more than five times in your life
- Sale of any illegal drug for profit
- Use of an illegal drug, no matter how many times or how long ago, while in a law-enforcement or prosecutorial position, or in

a position that carries with it a high level of responsibility or public trust

Applicants should also note that, by law, all Special Agents are subject to transfer at any time. This is a condition of employment, and while personal preferences and family issues are considered where possible, failure to accept a transfer can be grounds for dismissal.

Weight and Health

Likewise, the job description for the Special Agent position notes that "a Special Agent must be fit for strenuous physical exertion." The FBI requires that applicants meet certain physical standards. Males cannot exceed 19 percent body fat and females cannot exceed 22 percent. There are also weight criteria that must be observed. These are as follows:

Males		Females	
5'4"	117–163	5'0"	96–138
5'5"	120–167	5'1"	99–141
5'6"	124–173	5'2"	102–144
5'7"	128–178	5'3"	105–149
5'8"	132–183	5'4"	108–152
5'9"	136–187	5'5"	111–156
5'10"	140–193	5'6"	114–161
5'11"	144–198	5'7"	118–165
6'0"	148–204	5'8"	122–169
6'1"	152–209	5'9"	126–174
6'2"	156–215	5'10"	130–179
6'3"	160–220	5'11"	134–185
6'4"	169–231	6'0"	138–190
6'5"	174–238		

An applicant's medical history is examined closely for any medical condition or history that could affect the individual's ability to perform the duties of Special Agent. Although the applicant's doctor may certify that he or she is capable of meeting the required physical demands of the position, this determination can be made only by the FBI's chief medical officer. The FBI does not automatically disqualify those with disabilities from applying for the Special Agent position, but it will carefully evaluate those conditions.

Applicants must have uncorrected vision not worse than 20/200 (Snellen) and corrected vision of 20/20 in one eye and not worse than 20/40 in the other eye. Persons who have had laser surgery must wait one year from the date of the surgery and produce documentation as to the results of the procedure and also the recovery of the eye tissue.

Qualifying Tests

Applicants are invited to take a battery of tests and, in some cases, such as language program applicants, they take specialized tests in the field of expertise. These tests are designed to judge cognitive function and situational reasoning. There are two phases to the testing process.

Note: Some military veterans may qualify for veteran's preference in the testing procedure. Having veteran status will not affect the test scores, but veterans are given preference in being allowed to sit for the tests. Those seeking to avail themselves of this preference must present a valid form DD-214 during the application process. Persons who have questions about their eligibility for this preference, or those who cannot locate their form DD-214, should contact the nearest Department of Veteran's Affairs office.

Phase One Testing

Following FBI field office receipt of the online application, selected applicants are invited to take the Phase One tests at the field office that is processing the application. The Phase One tests take about three and one-half hours and are multiple choice. They test cognitive skills and also behavioral and situational judgment. The tests were developed by industrial occupational psychologists and are graded by FBI Headquarters on a pass–fail basis using algorithms. The field office processing the applications will be told who has passed or failed the tests. Approximately 65 percent of persons taking the Phase One test pass it. Those who do not are eligible to retake the tests, but they must wait at least one year before doing so.

Applicants should be aware that the FBI has somewhat strict rules for taking both the Phase One and later Phase Two tests. Notice of the tests is provided 30 days in advance. Tests are rarely rescheduled, so every effort must be made to make the appointed testing date. There are also items that applicants must not bring with them to the test sessions. These include the application brochure; any reference materials, such as dictionaries or textbooks; pens or pencils; reading material, such as books, magazines, or newspapers; work-related materials; briefcases; loose papers, or letters; beepers, pagers, or cellular telephones; or tape recorders, cassettes, compact disk players, calculators, or cameras. For those already employed in law enforcement or living in a state that permits the lawful carrying of concealed weapons, firearms may not be brought into an FBI facility.

Applicants should bring a current driver's license. If the driver's license does not have a photograph, another form of identification with a photograph must also be produced.

Once the testing is begun, applicants are not allowed to leave the area except for short, scheduled breaks that are on the FBI premises. Telephone calls are not allowed, nor is smoking or the use of smokeless tobacco. Time limits are strictly observed, and once testing has started, applicants may not speak to or with other applicants.

Applicants will be required to sign a nondisclosure form before taking each test and are strictly prohibited from discussing or disclosing the content of the tests either before or after taking them. Should a Special Agent applicant be hired and later found to have disclosed details about the tests to another applicant, the individual will be subject to disciplinary action, up to and including dismissal from the FBI.

Failure to comply with any of these rules may be the basis for immediate disqualification from consideration for the position.

Phase One Results

Based on the results of these tests, applicants are asked to complete form SF-86, Questionnaire for National Security Positions. The manner in which this nine-page form is completed differs in the FBI. Other federal agencies ask for information in various categories for the past five years. The FBI requires these categories be completed back to age 18. Literally nothing is missed. Other than the obvious name, date, and place of birth, address, and telephone numbers, information is required on other names used; citizenship; places where you have lived; places where you have gone to school; employment history; persons who know you well; your spouse; relatives and associates; citizenship status of your relatives and associates; military history; foreign countries you have visited; your activities in those countries; your selective service status; your police record; your use of illegal drugs and other drug-related activity; your use of alcohol; your record of investigations by other governmental agencies; your financial status; your litigation history; and your membership in groups or associations. Applicants are also asked to complete releases allowing the FBI to access financial, credit, medical, educational, employment, legal, professional, civil, criminal, and other records.

Some people believe that if they show a gap of more than a week or two between jobs, this will reflect badly on them and hurt their chances for positive consideration. If there is a logical explanation for a job gap (being unemployed for a period is not a crime), applicants should not attempt to cover up. The lapse will get discovered and call the applicant's candor into question. It is far better to state periods of unemployment and explain them in a forthright manner. Saying something to the effect of "I always wanted to live in Denver, so I moved there, but after three months I wasn't able to find a job I liked, so I moved back" is fine and much better than trying to pretend the three months never happened.

Applicants often do not get off to a good start in the application process when they return forms that are illegible, incomplete, or incorrect. This sloppiness slows down the application process and may actually hurt the applicant's candidacy if there is a suspicion of laziness, vagueness, deception, or lack of attention to detail. This form is, after all, being filled out by someone who alleges an interest in becoming an investigator in one of the most demanding agencies on the face of the earth. If the applicant cannot or will not complete the form in an accurate, timely manner, doubts are raised as to how well the person will do in the Special Agent position.

Completing the SF-86 may take some work. Old employers may have gone out of business or moved; dates of a foreign trip may be fuzzy; in-laws' addresses may be out of date; or a prior educational institution may have been consolidated into another entity. The time and effort is well spent, however. One is, after all, applying to be a federal investigator, so some legwork and telephone calls to clear up ambiguous areas is both needed and appropriate. When in doubt as to the completeness of a given portion of the questionnaire, or how some piece of needed information can be developed, it may be wise to contact one of the agents involved in the application process for guidance. This is preferable to turning in a seriously deficient questionnaire.

There are two other reasons the applicant would do well to respect the completion of the SF-86 in the required manner. Every statement and fact on the form will be checked twice: once during a polygraph examination and again during the full field background investigation. If there are errors, evasions, or acts of omission, they will be detected and will do little to advance your candidacy.

In 2005, the FBI estimated that it would test about 12,000 applicants in Phase One tests. Only about 2,500 would be nominated to take the Phase Two test. Thus, the winnowing process begins.

Phase Two Testing

The individual field offices nominate applicants for Phase Two testing based on a number of factors. As noted, the FBI hires out of the applicant categories, and each field office has an allotment from each category. Thus, for example, Kansas City, Missouri, may have a yearly allotment of four applicants from the science category, two from engineering, seven from accounting/financial, and so on. It is up to the applicant recruiter or coordinator in each office to nominate the most competitive candidates from each category. This decision is reviewed and approved by more senior officials in the field office and then the nominations are forwarded to FBI Headquarters. Prior to making these nominations, the applicant recruiter or coordinator meets with each applicant and ascertains the following information:

- Are you available to take the Phase Two examination during a set period in the future?
- If you pass Phase Two, can you accept a Special Agent position within 90 days after being notified of the test results?
- Can you report for duty with two weeks' notice, if selected?
- Do you understand that you must be available for transfer to meet the needs of the Bureau?

The applicant coordinator or recruiter also discusses with the applicant the requirements of the Special Agent position, the possibility that the applicant will be required to use deadly force, the demands of New Agents Training, the pay and benefits pertaining to the Special Agent position, and other pertinent matters.

Based on this field-level selection process, each field office nominates candidates to FBI Headquarters for Phase Two testing. These nominations are received at FBI Headquarters in a blind fashion. That is, they are reviewed with no information that would identify the applicant's name, gender, or ethnicity. The candidates are then rated by a Headquarters review board and the field offices are notified of who has been approved to proceed to Phase Two testing.

The first stage of Phase Two testing is a panel interview, during which the applicant appears before a panel of Special Agents who have been specially trained in selection interviewing. Panel interviews are held in six field offices: Cleveland, Kansas City, Phoenix, Baltimore, Philadelphia, and Miami. The FBI pays travel expenses for applicants to appear for their interviews. Business attire is expected when appearing for a panel interview and, indeed, it is not a bad idea at the Phase One testing stage.

The interview takes one hour, and there are no trick or spontaneous questions. The interviewing agents ask 14 standardized, behaviorally based questions that have been developed with the assistance of outside consultants. Among the objectives of the interview are to assess the applicant as to the following criteria:

Ability to communicate orally
Ability to organize, plan, and prioritize
Ability to relate effectively to others
Ability to maintain a positive image
Ability to evaluate information and make judgments
Initiative and motivation
Ability to adapt to changing situations
Integrity
Physical requirements

Following the interview there is a 1½-hour essay-type exercise in which the applicant writes a summary or report of an imaginary investigation. The objective is to test the applicant's cognitive and communications skills. Specifically, it assesses the applicant's ability to communicate effectively, to attend to details, and to evaluate and make judgment decisions. At this time, the essays are hand-written. The essays are graded by an alternate set of Special Agent assessors in the field office. Grading is done against a standard checklist, and the agents on the interviewing panel have no input into the grading of the essay. They do score the interview, but do not know what the passing score is. They merely report the score to FBI Headquarters. About 50 percent of applicants pass Phase Two testing.

It is important to note that an applicant cannot, under current

FBI policy, completely fail one portion of Phase Two testing and make the deficiency up with stellar performance on another portion.

The Final Steps

FBI Headquarters notifies the field offices as to which applicants passed Phase Two testing. At this point, a fairly intensive series of events begins. The applicant is scheduled for a physical examination, paid for by the FBI. The applicant is also fingerprinted and these fingerprints are checked against FBI and other governmental fingerprint repositories. The applicant takes a drug test and is given a security interview. The latter is designed to ensure that the applicant has no potential problems with being granted future access to highly classified information. Also, at this point, the full field background investigation is begun, using the information provided on the form SF-86. There is also a polygraph examination.

The idea of taking a polygraph examination is daunting to some applicants, but it need not be. The examination is painless, and unlike how it may be portrayed in books and movies, is not some form of voodoo. It is simply a time-tested technique to measure physiological responses to questions. The theory is simple. Persons who lie exhibit different physical responses to questions than do people who do not lie. The machine tests breathing, pulse, and electric conductivity of the skin.

The machine is only a tool, and it is the professional examiner with years of training and experience who picks up the patterns that are indicative of deception. While there are some books and movies that claim to offer methods to "beat" the polygraph, they are essentially useless and may actually produce the result they are intended to mask—deception. If an applicant has been truthful and candid in the application process and the completion of the SF-86, the polygraph examination is a minor inconvenience. The tests usually take 30 minutes to an hour.

Applicants who pass Phase Two testing have, in essence, been conditionally "hired." That is, the FBI has decided that they want this person as a new agent trainee, contingent upon the results of the medical examination, the polygraph examination, and the background investigation. There is no guarantee that an appointment letter will be forthcoming, even if all results are positive, as circumstances and budgets can always change, but the FBI has in essence targeted this applicant for a slot in a future new agents class.

In short, to be offered an appointment, there must be a vacancy in the critical skills category you are applying for. Thus, for example, if the FBI had 900 Special Agent slots to fill in a given fiscal year and had allotted 100 of them for persons with CPAs, one of these slots would have to be open for an applicant in the accounting/finance category to be offered an appointment. In situations such as this, when the candidate has passed Phase Two testing, the FBI might hold off beginning the full field background investigation until the beginning of the next fiscal year. This way the promising applicant could be slotted against a new fiscal year's approved hiring positions. The FBI fiscal year starts October 1.

People—Where Wins and Losses Happen

To be realistic, most people who want to be FBI agents, no matter how badly or for how long, do not make it. That is a simple fact of life in a very competitive environment. Some people have grades that are not good enough, while others have career and life experiences that do not measure up. Then there are those with medical problems that come up in their background investigation. Others may have excellent credentials in an academic or professional field that simply is not high enough on the Bureau's roster of current needs.

Others, however, can be quite competitive in every way and still not make the cut because they enter the application process with preconceived notions as to what the FBI is about and what it wants. Oftentimes, these notions come as a result of media portrayals that are severely flawed. These are tragic losses, mainly because with a little thought and preparation on the part of the applicant, they could be avoided. This chapter provides an overview of the process and offers some tips on making the application process a personal success.

One Very Long Interview

While there is a fair amount of paperwork involved in applying to become an FBI agent, keep one thing foremost in your mind: it is really one very long interview. It will take place over a period of weeks or months, it will be in person and over the telephone, and it will be somewhat formal at times and somewhat informal at other times. Part of the process is planned that way and part of it is just the normal give and take that comes with finding out about a new career choice.

At each step, the interviewing agents, often led by the applicant coordinator in the field office, are forming impressions about you. Are you professional? Well spoken? Punctual? Accurate? Thorough? Dependable? Biased? Arrogant? Articulate? Honest? Decisive? Well informed? Intuitive? Well reasoned? Bright? The list could go on, but the point is obvious. There are roughly 70 applicants for each Special Agent position. These agents are trying to determine who will be the best candidate, beyond grades and resume, and these interactions are chock full of clues. Rarely does the FBI chase an applicant because of his or her unique background. The reverse is almost always the case: the FBI has to turn down many good people to make sure those it selects are worthy of the opportunity.

First impressions count. In discussing the cover letters they receive, employers estimate that 85 percent of them are so sloppy, flawed, inaccurate, or incomplete that they fail to generate the opportunity for an interview. Successful job applicants spend four or even five hours reviewing and polishing their cover letters and then have them reviewed by friends and associates. The point is that the cover letter is your chance to make a solid first impression, be it by letter, e-mail, telephone call, or in person. So make it count.

This is not to suggest that you try to act a part during the application process; precisely the opposite is the case. *You should be yourself.* But the application process is also not the place to try out ethnic humor or brag about how well your father knows Senator So-and-So. Neither is it the time for false humility. The FBI wants bright, successful people for a very simple reason; they tend to make bright, successful agents. So let the facts speak for themselves and be yourself. There is no need to force your personality and resume into some sort cookie-cutter mold in the hope it will resemble the prototypical FBI agent. There is no such thing in reality, and besides, the FBI needs and seeks a diverse workforce.

That presenting yourself accurately is so crucial is because the playing field here is severely tilted—in the interviewer's favor. The agents in the application process are professional law-enforcement officers who make their living interviewing people. They can read clues and body language, and also can spot a lie or an inconsistency at a thousand yards. They have tough, demanding jobs and they are not amused by people who miss appointments or cannot return paperwork in a reasonable time. They also have no tolerance for lies. An applicant caught lying might just as well tear up the application and walk out the door. Some people make this mistake of lying, and it is a foolish one. They think they have to be perfect to be accepted as an agent, so they distort some event in their past. They probably will get caught elsewhere in the application process or during the background. At this point, no amount of rationalizing or pleading or bluster will change the outcome. The moral of the story is simple: *do not lie.* Lies of commission—claiming something happened that did not—or of omission—failing to mention or note a pertinent fact—are equally disqualifying.

Experienced recruiters offer some basic tips for dealing with the interview. First, do your homework. Have some idea of what the employer is all about. Second, get organized and do some rehearsing. If there are three things you think make you a particularly attractive candidate, decide how you want to present them and in what order. Third, if you do not understand a question, ask for clarification. Trying to guess what someone is asking will almost always produce an incomplete or incomprehensible answer that will reflect poorly on your abilities.

Common sense should prevail. Show up on time. Wear appropriate business or business casual attire. Avoid extremes in cologne, makeup, fashion, and jewelry. Get a decent night's sleep the day before an appointment. Have an idea about what the FBI does; books and the FBI website are freely available, so check the Frequently Asked Questions section for information. Decide beforehand if you really want the job or if this is just a passing infatuation. Ask intelligent questions: anyone joining an outfit that carries guns and investigates terrorists would probably want to do that. Be polite and professional. Do not yammer on about how many FBI movies you have seen and how cool you thought they were. The interviewing agent either has not seen them or has and is not impressed with their content. (*The Silence of the Lambs* may be an exception; it was very well done and, with some artistic exceptions, was fairly accurate.)

Applicants are also well advised to avoid what, for lack of a better term, could be called "Rambo syndrome." Excessive questions about weapons, FBI shooting policies, or statements about how tough you are and how willing you are to be involved in dangerous confrontations will only raise more questions than they answer. The FBI and, for that matter any law-enforcement agency, is wary of applicants who think the position involves lots of car chases and shoot-outs.

Early Contacts

One of the most effective steps you can take is to meet some FBI agents even before entering the application process. Such a meeting may be useful in deciding if this is your career path of choice or not. Meeting agents is not as difficult as you might think. FBI agents are hardly invisible; indeed, it is part of their mission to educate the public about the Bureau's roles and responsibilities. Numerous Bureau personnel, to include SACs, ASACs, supervisors, and even street agents in field offices, make speeches all the time to business, civic, and professional groups. With a little research you should be able to find one or more of these events. You might even call the field office, ask for the media relations representative, and check if there are any public speeches scheduled in the near future. Explain that you are interested in joining the Bureau, might want to apply for the Special Agent position, and would like to learn a little more about the organization.

When you attend the event, listen to the presentation, then go up after the speech and introduce yourself. Explain that you have been considering the Special Agent position and wondered if the speaker had a few moments to chat. Be prepared to ask some questions such as those listed below later, but remember this is also your first "interview," if brief and informal. Wear attire appropriate for the occasion. If alcohol is served at the function, be moderate in terms of consumption.

While this course of action is recommended, do not overdo it unless the agent happens to be a friend or a friendship develops on the basis of that first meeting. It is fine to go to one or two public appearances, but showing up repeatedly will begin to raise suspicions that you are a "buff." Buffs are as old as law enforcement itself. They are people who are fascinated by law enforcement and like to hang around law-enforcement officers. They usually are harmless, but are viewed as a nuisance by most law-enforcement professionals.

Another way to meet an agent is through the old standby, networking. If you know, or know of, a state or local law-enforcement officer or prosecutor, that individual probably knows one or more agents and can perhaps arrange a meeting. So, too, with local attorneys, bankers, religious leaders, and other professionals you know. Many such people are contacted on a somewhat regular basis by agents in the course of their duties, or they may belong to social or professional groups in which an agent is a member. Many agents are physical fitness enthusiasts and frequent sports clubs near their FBI field office. Contacts at, or membership in, these clubs can spur contacts.

Another venue is your college alumni relations office. A quick phone call can probably help you determine if any recent alumni are FBI agents, even if they are now assigned to a distant city. A phone call to one of them is made easier by the fact that you both went to the same school, albeit probably at different times. Even a phone conversation is a start toward gaining an appreciation of what the FBI and the Special Agent position are all about, and it is likely the agent can refer you to someone in your local field office for a possible personal meeting.

Should these efforts yield results, make the first person-to-person meeting a light one—perhaps a cup of coffee or lunch in a local diner. Dinner is probably a bit much at this early stage. The objective is to start the process, then see where it leads.

Other Ways to Make Contact with Agents

A more structured opportunity to meet Special Agents, especially if you are still in college, is to attend one of the many career fairs in which the FBI participates each year. In 2005, the FBI took part in well over one hundred such events in 27 states. While most of these events were linked to colleges and universities, a number were sponsored by cities and regions, professional associations, or ethnic groups. A bit of research on the FBI website can produce a list of such events with little effort. Indeed, the website should be a frequent resource for serious applicants. It is literally possible to spend days on the site, learning about the history of the Bureau, its organization and structure, its mission, its field offices, the history of women in the FBI, and much more. An excellent search engine allows you to browse thousands of topics and learn things about the Bureau that even some veteran FBI agents do not know.

While such events are a good first step to actually meet an agent, they tend to be crowded, so your ability to ask detailed questions about the Special Agent position may be limited. If you are seeking to maximize your time with the agent, you might want to arrive just as the event begins or ask the agent if it would be possible to call at a later date to do some follow-up. If you are going to attend one of these events, keep in mind that this is a first-impression opportunity and dress accordingly. It is likely the agent will be wearing a suit. If you are on a college campus, it is not necessary to show up wearing a suit, however, choose neat, clean, and moderate clothing to make that positive first impression.

Many FBI field offices also conduct "citizen's academies," which are weeks- or months-long programs designed to introduce members of the public to facets of the FBI's mission and organization. These academies may meet, for example, one afternoon a week for eight weeks, with each meeting devoted to a different FBI investigative program. There is no set design to the academies, so the wise applicant would do well to inquire of the local FBI field office to determine if such events are offered and how to go about applying.

Appropriate Questions

In the course of your investigation, there will be opportunities to ask questions of the agents you speak with. Indeed, the agents may ask you to pose questions. Some common sense and a little preparation can make this process both informative and beneficial. A few typical questions might include:

- How long have you been in the Bureau?
- What sorts of assignments have you had?
- What do you find most rewarding about the position?
- How did you find New Agents Training?
- Is there anything you recommend to improve my chances of success in New Agents Training?
- What was the most difficult adjustment you had to make in assuming the agent position?
- How has your family adapted to your being an agent?

While hardly exhaustive or profound, questions of this type are logical and insightful. They are suggestive of an applicant who has thought through the potential transition to a new career shared by very few others. They also evidence a concentration on the job itself, and not concerns with its peripheral elements.

While there may be "good" questions during the applicant process, there are also "bad" ones. A few examples include:

- Do I have to work nights or weekends?
- If I am on vacation and something big happens, will I be called back?
- Do I have to wear a suit all the time?
- How quickly can I be promoted?
- How much vacation will I get?
- What kind of guns do you guys carry?
- Did you ever shoot anybody?

In short, the advice is to show a sincere interest in wanting the job and in trying to understand its important elements. Issues like time off and vacation days are worthwhile, but the early stages of the application process are probably not the time to ask them. Likewise, the guns and danger stuff, at least in the early stages, should be off-limits. One need not be obsequious, but some common sense is always in order. Be aware also that some phases of the interview process are more conducive to interaction with the processing agents than other phases. For example, during the Phase Two testing, opportunities for interaction are very limited.

Realistic Expectations

It is important to grasp a very simple but often overlooked fact of life. This is an age of increasing specialization, when the FBI is seeking computer scientists, foreign language speakers, and engineers, among other skill sets. Somewhat frequently, applicants display a keen interest in maintaining their professional credentials after they become an agent. They ask whether the FBI will pay for them to maintain their certifications, allow them time off to do so, and the like. The FBI is pro-training, and spends a lot of time and money to ensure its agents are well equipped to do their jobs. It is not, however, in the business of professional development. The computer scientist (or engineer or language speaker) coming on board will not be a computer scientist who also happens to be an FBI agent. Rather, the individual will be an FBI agent who happens to have a background in computer science.

For many, the change in personal perspective is not difficult and the rewards of the FBI work are immense. In a recent news story on Special Agents Sung-Li Lim and Sang Jun, both highly trained and well-compensated computer specialists prior to their joining the FBI, these agents explained that they found the technical challenges of doing computer-related investigations in the Bureau easily equal to and, in many ways, superior to the experiences they had in the private sector, where they certainly made more money. But this trade-off may not be the best for everyone. Especially if you are in a technical field, it is critical that you be realistic about your choice of an FBI job.

The demands of being an agent will, absent truly unusual circumstances, always overshadow your particular educational and professional background. Down the road, the Bureau may ask you, now that you have some investigative experience under your belt, to assume duties for which your specialized background will be very important. Indeed, that may be the reason you were selected in the first place, but it is not the primary reason in the early stage of your career.

It is also important to note that you will have almost no ability to dictate the type of work to which you will be assigned. While your educational or professional background may suit you well for certain types of work, the FBI makes its work assignments based on a series of factors, of which educational and professional background is but one piece. For example, you may have a prodigious background in technology and wind up working organized crime cases in Cleveland. With time and experience, and several years' satisfactory service as an investigator, you may be able to request reassignment to a line of work of more interest to you, but this option rarely is granted to fairly new agents.

Some applicants, perhaps too eager to impress, overplay their hands, and it shows fairly quickly. Statements like, "I've dreamed about being an agent since I was ten" are fine, if true, but raise the logical question, "So what have you been doing about it?" One would assume if the agent position were a lifetime goal, there would be some evidence of that; for example, the individual would have researched the history and responsibilities of the Bureau and its hiring requirements, and be fairly knowledgeable about recent items in the press. If not, then it is probably wise to tone down the enthusiasm.

Missteps in the Application Process

The applicant process raises an issue that is an important distinction between the private and public sectors: *negotiation*. Negotiation is a way of life in the private sector—we negotiate car and home prices, sales goals, commission and bonus calculations, office transfers, and much more. In the public sector, and especially in the FBI application process, negotiation is an unknown. The FBI has the ability to negotiate almost nothing, except perhaps the date of entry or duty, if one is accepted. The Bureau cannot negotiate salary, office of assignment, vacation days, or any other terms of employment, and efforts to do so are futile.

Generally speaking, it is better to have a job during the application process. There are a number of reasons for this. First, your effort to be selected as an FBI agent may not be successful. Second, the application process can take many months, and it helps to be employed. Third, an employed person making application may look more sincere than someone who needs a job—perhaps any job.

There is a question that is double-edged. It is appropriate, logical, and needed; but phrased in the wrong way or asked at the wrong time, it can create a negative impression: How long does the application process take?

The question itself is fine, and you would be a fool not to ask it at some point. There are real-world interests involved. You have a job, you may be expecting a promotion or transfer, you may be adding a child to your family, you may have sick parents. *Timing* can be important. You do not, however, want to create the impression that you are interested in the job only within a certain time frame—unless that is literally true. And the reason for this may not be immediately apparent to the agent.

The agents handling the application process have very little control over when you will be hired, assuming you are selected. They can only recommend candidates to FBI Headquarters where the selections are made. Then, even after you have been selected, classes must be formed. This, again, can affect timing. There may be other issues, as well. If there are medical conditions to be evaluated, these could slow the application process, as could questions that emerge during the background investigation.

The agents processing your application may be able to give you a probable range for entering, should you be selected, but that is about as good as they can do, and even that is an educated guess. Some, rather than offer a date that may be wrong, avoid providing any data. Candidates who create the impression that they are interested only if they can begin on a certain date or certain month may hurt their chances for positive consideration.

Other Considerations Regarding Application

It is at this early point in the application process that you should begin to give substantial thought to the family implications of a career as an FBI agent. A real-life example may be illustrative:

Some years back, a very promising applicant who was a law-enforcement officer was offered an appointment as an agent. The person accepted and did very well in New Agents Training, being at the top of his class in almost every subject and practical problem. When he got his first office assignment in the sixth week of the training cycle, he discovered that the state to which he was going to be assigned could be a problem for his wife, a registered nurse. She was licensed in their home state and made almost twice as much as her husband. However, the new state to which he was to be posted would not accept her credentials until she had completed almost a year of additional training and certification. The financial impact of the transfer caused the new agent to drop out.

Perhaps nothing could have been done to remedy this unfortunate situation, but perhaps something could have been done. The new agent, after consultation with his spouse, could have selected FBI offices in states for assignment where his wife's credentials would be readily transferable. There would be no guarantee that this strategy would have worked, but it would certainly increase the chances for a positive resolution. One may be tempted to ask, when this situation came to light, why the FBI did not amend the orders of this promising young agent to a state where the spouse's license would not be an issue. The probable answer is simple: litigation. The FBI has been the subject of lawsuits alleging disparate treatment in personnel issues and, unfortunately, has had to become less flexible lest it foster more legal action.

Again, the important factor is consultation. The new agent is not the only one being transferred; the entire family is, and there is ample time to have these discussions. In response to situations such as this, the Bureau has made an interview with the applicant's spouse part of the application process.

Another factor is important at this stage of the applicant process: availability. Filling FBI new agent classes is a complicated and competitive process. Invariably, some promising new agents, having been offered an appointment, decline for professional or personal reasons. Sometimes, this can occur on fairly short notice. An applicant who has the ability to accept an appointment on fairly short notice may be selected to fill one of these vacancies, thus improving their chances of making the cut. Persons who have passed Phase Two testing are well advised to let their processing agents know how to get in touch with them if they are on vacation or out of town on personal or business travel.

Alternatives to Consider

Some persons seek to become FBI agents by more circuitous routes. For example, for many years the FBI has had an Honors Intern program at Headquarters. Each year about 50 college students are brought into these paid positions and they work alongside veteran FBI employees in administrative and analytical positions. Generally, these positions are open to students who are between their junior and senior years in college, or between their senior year and a graduate school into which they have already been accepted. Prior service as an Honors Intern does not exempt an applicant from having to be otherwise qualified and competitive, but the prior experience does not hurt, either.

In addition to the Honors Intern program, the FBI has a number of unpaid intern positions in the following units:

• *Special Agent Applicant Processing Unit.* Positions in this unit offer the student an opportunity to assist in the FBI hiring process and help research applicant processing and human resources management.

• *Headquarters Personnel Resources Unit.* Positions in this unit offer the student an opportunity to earn academic credit while assisting the FBI in monitoring and developing recruiting, testing, and interviewing initiatives.

• *Headquarters Performance Recognition and Awards Unit.* Positions in this unit offer the student the opportunity to earn academic credits while assisting the FBI human resources function in managing and implementing employee recognition programs. The FBI tries to ensure that exceptional performance is recognized through both monetary and honorific awards in both its Special Agent and support populations.

• *National Center for the Analysis of Violent Crime (NCAVC).* Positions in this unit offer the student the opportunity to observe and assist as the NCAVC provides investigative support to law-enforcement agencies around the world in regard to murder, arson, serial rape, child abduction or exploitation, terrorism, bombing, and other cases. Services include offender research, profiling unknown offenders, threat assessment, crime analysis, investigative strategies, and prosecutorial assistance.

• *FBI Academy.* Positions at the academy involve the student in the operation and development of the FBI's core training function for Special Agent and law-enforcement personnel. There are multiple intern positions available at Quantico and interns there not only get to see new agents going through their training cycles but also get to interact with the FBI instructors teaching them. There is perhaps no better venue to gain a rapid appreciation of what New Agents Training is all about.

In addition to the FBI programs, there are Presidential Management Fellows Programs for those with more advanced degrees. Created in 1977, these positions are two-year, paid opportunities to attract to the federal service applicants with outstanding academic credentials. These positions can transform into permanent federal government employment.

If you are interested in an intern position, apply early. Since interns will have access to FBI facilities and information, applicants must have a full field background investigation completed before they can begin service. This requires completion of form SF-86, Questionnaire for National Security Positions. The form, which is discussed in some detail in Chapter 6, can be a chore to complete.

For those who apply for the Special Agent position and are not competitive, often because of a relative lack of experience, the negative result is not the end of the line. You can apply for other federal investigative jobs where your credentials are apt to be more competitive. If hired, you will gain valuable experience as an investigator, then you can later apply again to the FBI. If you subsequently are accepted, you will still have to go through New Agents Training, but you will be given vacation and retirement credit for your service in the other agency. If you are contemplating this path, there is one important distinction. Within the federal civil service, all jobs are given numbers. FBI Agents are 1811s, as are Secret Service agents, agents of the Drug Enforcement Administration, and scores of other federal law-enforcement personnel. Generally, these personnel are armed and have powers of arrest. There are, however, other investigator positions within the federal civil service who, while conducting investigations, are not armed, and do not have powers of arrest. These are 1810 positions. While both forms of experience will be useful in competition for the Special Agent position, only service in an 1811 position will transfer into the Bureau and count toward a law-enforcement retirement. The other service counts for salary, basic retirement, and vacation purposes, but not toward 1811 retirement, which has a higher calculation.

You might also seek to gain relevant experience through service in state or local law-enforcement agencies. This experience is deemed valuable by the Bureau and may make you a more competitive candidate down the road, although the time served with the state or local agency will not transfer to the federal system. Again, if accepted by the FBI, you will have to go through New Agents Training.

Still other applicants decide to apply for FBI support positions. There are a number of advantages to this strategy, especially if you are young or are not competitive because you lack relative work experience. To come into the FBI as a support employee you will have to make a separate application and will be subject to the same full field background investigation that agent applicants undergo. You may apply for a position at FBI Headquarters or a field office. While either provides great insight into what the FBI is all about, working in a field office affords the best view of what FBI agents actually do for a living.

Some support employees continue their schooling while they work for the Bureau, while some come to the Bureau straight out of high school, then complete their college education while employed in a support position. This is possible because most support positions have fairly normal business hours, thereby allowing classroom time in the evening.

At one point in its history, the FBI gave preference to support employees applying for the agent position, and many agents came up through this route. This practice was discontinued several decades ago, but employment as a support employee still offers a number of advantages. For example, support employees still can become agents, but they must compete with non-Bureau candidates in the various hiring categories the FBI has established for agent applicants. There are other advantages, too. For example, the pay as a support employee is roughly comparable to that available for equivalent positions in the private sector. Second, there is no better or more effective way to learn about the FBI and what FBI agents do. Third, you will be working with agents who can make positive recommendations to those involved in the agent selection process. Fourth, if you are ultimately accepted as a new agent, all prior Bureau service carries forward for retirement, vacation, and pay purposes. It does not, however, count toward the number of years needed to qualify for the law-enforcement portion of the retirement computation. Fifth, being employed in certain types of support positions—such as intelligence analysis, financial analysis, or special surveillance—may qualify you for one or more new agent hiring categories.

Still other applicants choose to remain in their current jobs or seek employment in a challenging, but unrelated, field. If you do so, and move into managerial or supervisory ranks with your employer, or gain valuable technical experience that makes you more competitive as a Special Agent applicant, you can reapply to the FBI.

Conclusion

All in all, the application process can be a lengthy and sometimes frustrating affair. The Bureau has worked to improve it for many years, and much progress has been made, but the need to select one person out of roughly every 70 applicants can never be made easy or fast. Patience is a virtue.

CHAPTER
8

New Agents Training

A visit to the FBI Academy starts in an almost pedestrian manner. You turn off of Interstate 95 about 40 miles south of Washington, D.C., at a sign for the Marine Corps Base–Quantico, and you begin to drive along a two-lane blacktop road through the wooded hills of northern Virginia. Almost immediately, on the right, there is a discreet entrance to a national military cemetery, but other than that there is little evidence of a military presence. That quickly changes, however.

The Academy Surroundings

One of the most distinctive attributes of this ordinary stretch of blacktop headed to the FBI Academy is its speed limit signs. The speed limit changes six or seven times in the space of six miles. The lower limits are to protect troops marching along the shoulder of the highway from training area to training area. Traffic is the normal mix of civilian cars, with the occasional military vehicle passing by. About a mile and a half down this road, the situation changes dramatically. You encounter a U.S. Marine Corps checkpoint staffed with fit, lean, polite, young Marines toting automatic weapons. They are invariably cordial, overly courteous (get used to being called "Sir" or "M'am"), curious, and deadly serious. You do not drop in unannounced at the U.S. Marine Corps Base–Quantico—or the FBI Academy, for that matter. Photo identification and the reason for your visit are quickly produced.

Once through the Marine Corps checkpoint, you continue your journey along the blacktop, but the military presence quickly increases. You pass a Marine Corps firestation on your left (yes, the Marines have firefighters—civilian personnel with red trucks), and shortly thereafter a vehicle repair depot. Soon, on the right, is an ammo storage area, with a red flag always flying to designate the presence of explosive ordinance. Behind a large fence and rows of barbed wire reside numerous bunkers dug into the earth, holding unimaginable amounts of ammunition and other forms of military ordinance.

It is in many ways fitting that the FBI Academy is on a Marine Corps base, for the institutions are remarkably similar in many ways. Each is but a small part of a much larger component. The Marine Corps is part of the U.S. Navy, and the FBI is part of the U.S. Department of Justice. Each has a unique identity and persona that it guards intensely. Each is a demanding environment, chockfull of myths and legends. Each is highly selective about who it recruits. Each has a demanding training cycle and little tolerance for deviance from its rules and regulations. Each has a loyal corps of alumni who are ardent in their feelings for the institution. Each is looked to by the citizens of the United States to perform difficult, complex, and dangerous missions. And, each is not everyone's cup of tea.

The relationship between the FBI and the Marine Corps goes back to the 1930s, when the FBI Academy was first founded at Quantico. At that time it was little more than a few small buildings and several firearms ranges. The vast majority of training was conducted in Washington, D.C., with agents coming to Quantico only several times in their training cycle for firearms training. The modern FBI Academy dates to 1972, and has even expanded significantly since then.

A little further down the road, again on the right, is a Marine

Corps' sniper training range, with targets so far downrange they look little bigger than dimes. On this range, Marine snipers routinely put shots in a target area the size of a volleyball from hundreds and hundreds of yards away. Then, on the right, is the entrance to the FBI Academy. Once again, there is a checkpoint, manned by FBI police. The FBI has its own police force, with uniforms, firearms, badges, and police cars emblazoned with "FBI Police" on the sides. These personnel are nonagents, but nonetheless are sworn, federal law-enforcement officers, charged with protecting FBI facilities and personnel. Again, photo identification is inspected and the purpose of your visit is ascertained.

You are then on your own—at least for a bit. The next stop is the visitor registration desk on the ground floor of the Jefferson Dormitory. Once again, the purpose of your visit is ascertained and photo identification produced, but this time when you are granted a visitor's badge, your identification is held, to be returned when you turn in your visitor's badge upon departure. There are no unescorted visitors to the FBI Academy; even retired Special Agents must have an escort at all times. A call is made to your host, and you wait in the open, airy lounge.

More than a College Campus

At this point, you begin to get a sense of what the FBI Academy (or "Quantico," as agents call it) is all about. First, the setting reminds you of any small college campus, with a few pronounced exceptions. The 11 buildings are brick and all are connected by glass-enclosed walkways. It is possible to walk the better part of a quarter mile, from building to building, and never go outside. There are two reasons for this. First, students are not exposed to bad weather when navigating between classes. Second, security is tighter with only a few controlled entrances.

Other signs convey a sense of small-town college life. There is a bulletin board crammed with flyers from local hotels announcing special weekend rates, names of area florists (yes, even FBI agents send flowers to loved ones), ads for rental car companies, and notices of companies offering shuttle service to local airports. Somewhat prominent is a flyer for FERCAT, which is a feral cat catch and release program started by FBI employees. The flyer announces proudly that in the nine years the program has been in existence, 82 cats have been caught, neutered, and placed for adoption. And of course volunteers are sought. Other posters announce blood drives, movie offerings, service schedules at local houses of worship, and retirement/promotion parties.

The FBI Academy occupies 385 acres on the sprawling 60,000-acre Marine Corps base, and in many ways is a small town unto itself. But it's a somewhat unusual town. One thing that strikes you immediately is the frequent sound of gunfire. Somewhere on the academy grounds for much of the workday someone is firing something, be it a pistol, shotgun, rifle, or submachine gun. Occasionally, there is the loud boom of explosives being set off by SWAT teams or the Hostage Rescue Team. Other times, there is the rolling thunder sound of heavy ordinance being detonated by the Marine Corps some distance away. Then there are the helicopters. Throughout the day, they zoom or hover overhead, ferrying students into or out of practical problems or providing airborne surveillance for other exercises.

There is ample parking for all categories of students immediately adjacent to the Jefferson Dormitory, and a slow ride through the parking lot will reveal license plates from almost every state, often attached to police cruisers and vehicles. A huge FBI Command Vehicle—once a fire truck and reportedly worth almost half a million dollars—sits in a corner of the parking lot, awaiting deployment to support an FBI operation.

The next thing your mind absorbs is color. The FBI Academy is a riot of colors, with each category of student wearing a different-colored shirt over khaki slacks: blue denotes FBI agent trainees; black is for agents and trainees of the Drug Enforcement Administration; and green is for students in the FBI National Academy, an advanced training program for local, state, federal, and foreign police officers. Other colors from special-purpose programs run at the academy only add to the mix. FBI instructors on field and practical problems wear gold shirts with the FBI logo on the left breast. Experienced agents attending in-service refresher training dress in business casual attire. Classroom instructors and higher ranking officials wear business suits.

Entering the academy proper offers an interesting mix of the routine and the unusual. Spacious lounges contain TV sets, video games, newspapers, and card tables. Some contain display cases with samples of elaborate and sometimes beautiful law-enforcement memorabilia from around the world, often donated by visiting students from other countries. Small alcoves contain coin-operated washers and dryers. There is even a Starbucks on campus, reportedly doing a brisk business. Vending machines abound, offering the usual mix of good and not-good-for-you fare. The hallways are adorned with artwork, often with a patriotic theme, and a quiet hush is the norm as people move about the campus.

At two locations along the hallways of the academy there are muted, but poignant, shrines to FBI agents and graduates of the FBI National Academy who gave their lives in the line of duty. The Hall of Honor, located near the chapel complex, is the larger of the two. It is not unusual to see individuals or small groups at these memorials, intently and silently studying the photographs and biographies of those honored, for they represent professionals who gave the last full measure in the performance of their duties.

The well-equipped, multistory library has a bank of computers where students and guests can check their e-mail or surf the Web, while still other computers offer access to the FBI's vast holdings of 45,000 items of law-enforcement literature. These resources include books, DVDs, audiobooks, videos, microfiche, and special collections. Generous selections of magazines and newspapers from around the world are easily accessed, while the stacks contain thousands of books on law enforcement and other subjects. There is also a holding of 10,000 government documents. The library is open 24 hours a day, seven days a week, and offers one-on-one instruction on the use of its computers and systems. There are numerous study tables interspersed among the stacks, and also study carrels available. Most books can be checked out and taken to rooms or lounges, if students prefer. There is no requirement that students purchase any study materials during training; everything they require is provided. The University of Virginia, which has had a decades-long association with the academy, has a continuing education office adjacent to the library.

Within the complex there is a bank, barbershop, pub, 1,000-seat auditorium/theater, post office, convenience store, laundry and dry cleaners, nurse and first-aid station, dining hall, chapel for multidenominational religious services, gym, pool, classrooms, and administrative offices. The dormitory is capable of accommodating about 900 students, housed two to a room with a private bath for each room. Closets are provided and "civilian" clothes are common and permitted. There is even a luggage storage facility to allow the students to better use their available closet space. The academy provides all linens, but does not offer alarm clocks or hangers. Students are advised to bring their own or purchase them at the on-site convenience store. Students with a telephone calling card can make unlimited calls from their rooms, but this is at their own expense. Often there is entertainment by local artists or even the instructional staff. Indeed, for many years a musical group composed of staff instructors performed gratis for various events under the highly appropriate name The Free Agents.

The cafeteria can seat several hundred persons at a sitting and offers foods and beverages at no cost to the student. Hours are varied to accommodate the fact that some students will be up early in the morning and others may be studying past the normal dinner hour. Cafeteria services are provided by an outside catering company under contract to the FBI, and efforts are made to introduce variety into the fare, as everyone realizes that four months of the same menu could get boring. Accordingly, several nights a month there are theme dinners, during which the menu is devoted to particular ethnic or regional foods. For those who want a break from cafeteria food, the adjacent pub offers café-style sandwiches, soups, and burgers at a modest cost. There are no private cooking facilities at Quantico, so there is no point in a student's preparing his own meals. The cafeteria, however, given the thousands of students it services each year from around the world, is highly experienced in dealing with special diets.

Should you want to get out for a break, remember that the academy is somewhat isolated. Assuming you are eligible to leave campus, it is about a 10-mile drive to the small town of Triangle, Virginia, located immediately outside the main gate of the Marine Corps base. There you can find the usual mixture of fast-food outlets along with a couple of decent restaurants. Several miles farther north on Route U.S. 1 from Triangle there are shopping malls with their normal mix of retail and food outlets.

One might think that the FBI Academy had a number of highly competitive athletic teams, judging from the number of well-developed individuals strolling through its hallways. While the academy encourages—yea, demands—a high level of physical fitness, many of the students and staff are especially serious about their workout programs, and it shows. There are some very athletic-looking people roaming these hallways; thank God, they are the good guys and women.

A Professional Ambience

As New Agent Trainees, prospective agents are treated in a polite, professional, yet demanding manner. There is no harassment or any sign of a boot-camp mentality. You might think of it more as a medical school, with scores of bright, motivated individuals being put through some very demanding paces on their way to a professional career. Students maintain their normal hair length and wear their normal amount of jewelry, consistent with what they might be doing. (Though, in some exercises, jewelry might pose a safety risk.) Women wear makeup and some men, even instructors, have mustaches. FBI New Agent Trainees do not march in formation; they walk, alone or in groups, from class to class. Backpacks and water bottles are ubiquitous, and the similarity to a college campus is heightened—except for the holsters hanging on every hip and the identification badges attached to belts and shirts.

Class sizes are about 30 to 50 individuals and questions are encouraged. FBI classes are full of former accountants, lawyers, doctors, pilots, bankers, managers, teachers, military officers, an occasional former nun or seminarian, scientists, realtors, a former pro athlete or two (for many years, Milt Graham, former lineman for the New England Patriots and a member of their Hall of Fame, was a highly respected agent in the New York Office of the FBI), law-enforcement officers, computer specialists, and more. There is even a former Grand Prix race-car driver who is an agent. These are bright, motivated people, and no effort is made to force rote material down their throats.

The average age of a New Agent Trainee is about 30. Indeed, the FBI prizes and seeks individuality and curiosity, since a bright, diverse, inquisitive, motivated workforce is essential to achieving its mission. As one long-time instructor noted, the ideal FBI agent is capable of operating on his own or as part of a team. Both skills are required in field work.

While FBI Agents start with a salary of about $49,000, this amount is supplemented significantly by locality and availability pay once they enter on duty in their first field office, with the result that their actual salary is around $60,000. After five years' service this amount is over $80,000 and can be higher if they have entered the Career Development Program. Even with these respectable numbers, it is still not uncommon for applicants to have taken a salary reduction of from $30,000 to $50,000 to enter on duty. These are people with a goal, and they are serious about it.

To support the notion that the FBI is an increasingly diverse place, the FBI announced in August 2004 the statistics that show such diversity among its staff: the total number of FBI employees was 28,576, of whom 12,156 were Special Agents; of the total employee base, nearly 16,000 were women or minorities; more than half of the Special Agent force have advanced degrees; more than 2,400 FBI employees are proficient in one or more foreign languages, and half of these are also agents.

Guidance Counselors

Each new class of agents has two volunteer field counselors assigned to it. The counselors are experienced agents from field offices around the country, and they live with the new agents in the dormitory for the 18 weeks of their training cycle. Each counselor is responsible for half the class, and he or she functions as a mentor, guide, coach, observer/evaluator, cheerleader, and if need be, disciplinarian. Counselors are literally available 24 hours a day, and they have separate rooms in which they can conduct discreet counseling sessions, work with a new agent on a subject the individual is having trouble mastering, or simply be a sounding board for whatever issues or problems may arise. Some counselors use this opportunity to get better acquainted with Quantico and decide they would like to apply for an instructor's position at some future point in their careers.

These counselors, and indeed the whole new agents class, report to a Supervisory Special Agent in the New Agent Training Unit. This position is held by an experienced Supervisory Special Agent whose responsibility it is to evaluate the New Agent Trainees and coordinate all aspects of their training.

The Training Contract

One of the first things a new agent trainee does upon arriving at the academy is to review and sign a contract. This document, 20 pages long, is not as imposing as its length might suggest. The contract is really just a reinforcement of what new agent applicants have been told throughout the application process. It is a contract between the new agent trainee and the FBI, with responsibilities on both sides.

First, there is formal notice that for the first 24 months of employment, to include the four months devoted to New Agents Training, the person is in a probationary status. The contract notes that for the first 12 months the agent will be evaluated on the performance of assigned duties and tasks. New agents will also, per the contract, be evaluated on their suitability for the Special Agent position throughout the 24-month probationary period.

The contract then notes that the purpose of New Agents Training is twofold: first, to teach the student the skills necessary to perform as an FBI agent; second, to assess the student's suitability to be an agent. This is done along six dimensions:

• *Conscientiousness.* New agents are expected to act in a responsible, thoughtful, dependable, and organized manner. Those who are unreliable, careless, negligent, or lax will not do well in the training cycle.

• *Cooperativeness.* New agents are expected to be capable of both following the chain of command and also working with others in a collaborative manner. This requirement reflects the need for those in law enforcement to be able to work with others in their agency and also with people from other agencies. Those who are disruptive, aloof, hard-headed, or insubordinate will not fare well in the FBI.

• *Emotional maturity.* Law-enforcement officers have a wide range of discretionary powers at their disposal, and they are expected to be judicious in how they use them. Behavior that is immature, excessive, immoral, passive, irrational, rigid, demeaning, harassing, or discriminatory will not be tolerated. Some might question why *passive* is included. Once you step into the world as an FBI agent, you are expected, by the FBI and the public, to know when to take action, as dictated by the circumstances.

• *Initiative.* The demands of the Special Agent position are hardly routine. Obstacles will be encountered. Criminals do not give up or identify themselves. Creativity, hard work, overcoming challenges, and going above and beyond expectations are required to perform successfully.

• *Integrity.* Without this essential quality, no one, no matter how well qualified, is fit to be an FBI agent. An agent's testimony in court can put someone in prison for the rest of his or her life. Agents hold top secret clearances and routinely have access to incredibly sensitive information. They encounter people who will offer bribes and inducements. They will often operate alone, when no one is looking to judge their behavior. Lying, cheating, stealing, dissembling, playing favorites, and abuse of governmental privileges is cause for serious disciplinary action.

• *Judgment.* While this dimension might at first glance appear to mirror that of emotional maturity, it adds a new element. This dimension is concerned with the new agent's ability to consider consequences, evaluate situations, think critically, deal with deficiencies, and accept criticism.

The contract then states the obvious: that any new agent trainee who is deemed to be substantially deficient in one or more of the above dimensions during the probationary period may be recommended for dismissal. When the student has completed the training, he or she is presumed to be a new agent who is fully capable of dealing with dangerous situations and bad people, but is also going to do that in a lawful, reasonable, and considerate manner.

While class sizes, as noted, are usually 30 to 50 students, on firearms exercises and practical problems, the instructor-to-student ratio is smaller, often approaching one-to-five. Sometimes this is for safety reasons and other times it is to make sure instructors are on hand to answer student questions. The idea is to achieve the greatest amount of knowledge transfer from experienced agents to trainees in the shortest period of time. It is not unusual for a student during a practical problem to ask variations on the same question two, three, or even four times. This is not interpreted that the student is slow to learn or hadn't studied the material, but rather, as an effort on his part to make sure he fully understands the issue at hand. This is when a close instructor–student ratio is essential.

The normal student day is from 8:00 A.M. to 5:00 P.M., but that can be illusory. Just as in medical school, students often get up early to study or work out, and many evenings after dinner they spend hours studying alone or in ad hoc groups. In reality, most students' days are from about 6:30 A.M. until 8:00 or 9:00 P.M. Students are restricted to campus the first two weeks of training, but thereafter they are free to leave between the hours of 5:00 P.M. and midnight. There is a midnight curfew, and it is enforced. Weekends likewise are free from 3:00 P.M. Friday until midnight Sunday. However, there is a catch, which brings to mind some valuable words of advice for the prospective trainee.

Pitfalls for Beginners

Old-time, experienced academy officials are able to reel off without hesitation the two most common mistakes new agent trainees make before arriving at Quantico. The first is not being in physical shape. There is a four-part physical fitness test that trainees must pass before they can graduate. The test consists of sit-ups, a 300-meter run, push-ups, and a 1½-mile run. A fifth event, pull-ups, is under evaluation and may be included in the future. The requirements are clearly spelled out in the application and pre-entry materials, and they are also discussed with applicants as part of the application process. Doing exceptionally well in one part of the test does not offset a failure in another part, so the test must be approached as whole.

Still, some new agent trainees show up at Quantico out of shape. They pay a penalty for this. There is really no reason for this, as the FBI provides a Pre-Quantico Kit that discusses physical training requirements and protocol, conditioning and stretching programs, and firearms training objectives and introductions. In fact, prior to being offered an appointment as a Special Agent, there is a physical fitness test administered at the FBI field office processing the new agent's application. Thus, not only is some level of fitness established early on, but prospective agents know what will be required of them at Quantico.

There is another physical fitness test during the first week of New Agents Training. Those who pass are allowed the off-campus privileges discussed above. Those who do not are restricted to campus until the seventh week of training in the hope that they will use the enforced time to log in some serious gym time to remedy their deficiencies. There is a second physical fitness test in the seventh week of training. Those who do not pass it are required to take another test in the 14th week of training. Absent a significant mitigating factor, such as injury, those failing the second fitness test are recommended for dismissal.

The second common mistake new agent trainees make is to underestimate the demands of the academic side of the training. As one senior official put it, "We cram four years of college into four months." Those who believe they can breeze through the training program without making a serious effort or devoting substantial time to mastering the subject matter are making a serious mistake. This often has family implications, as well. New agent trainees who think they are going to spend every weekend with their families may have a serious shock in store for them, even if their physical fitness levels have earned them the privilege. Obviously, people do take time off, and the FBI is reasonable about the need for time with families, but to underestimate the demands of the curriculum may cause grief in the long run.

A third, much less common reason for departure from the academy is separation anxiety or, put simply, homesickness. For some students, the academy represents the first time they have been apart from their families and loved ones for an extended period. Even being able to go off campus after the second week may be of little comfort if one's family is several thousand miles away. Throw in the stresses of the training regimen and some students decide the strain is simply too great. This is unfortunate, since a lot of their time and effort went into getting an appointment as a new agent, to say nothing of the financial outlay by the FBI in recruiting, processing, and selecting them. Students are well advised to discuss such matters in depth with those close to them prior to considering the FBI as a career.

New agents with other areas of potential weakness may benefit from being addressed, at least in part, before coming to the academy. If you are weak in basic computer skills, take a course or two before arriving to make the academy experience less stressful. The same is true of a more slippery skill set—people skills. FBI agents make their living dealing with people—asking questions, conducting interviews, securing the cooperation of witnesses, developing informants, dealing with prosecutors, making presentations, and working as part of a team. Basic people skills may be a tough subject to master in an academic environment, but there probably are courses available that will help you if you are "people-challenged" so you can cope more effectively with these demands. A lack of these people skills will certainly come out during the course of training, since some exercises are specifically designed to challenge you on these capabilities. For all the emphasis put on physical fitness, defensive tactics, and firearms skills, it is really reading, writing, and speaking skills that produce a superior agent.

Tests and Milestones

There are nine academic tests administered during the training cycle: two on legal issues, one on behavioral science, one on interviewing, one on ethics, two on basic and advanced investigative techniques, one on interrogation, and one on forensic science. Passing scores are 85 or better. Each trainee must pass each major examination before continuing. If students fail a test, they are counseled by the instructors and given an opportunity to review the materials in question. They can then take a make-up examination on substantially the same material. Two test failures will result in a recommendation for dismissal.

In addition, trainees must pass a defensive tactics test that involves elements of grappling and boxing, handcuffing, contact holds, searching subjects, weapons retention, and disarming techniques. While much emphasis is put on firearms training, use of less than lethal techniques is emphasized as a means of resolving incidents when possible.

For all the emphasis on firearms training, defensive tactics, and arrest techniques, the FBI is cognizant of the rights of citizens and noncitizens alike with whom agents will come in contact with in the course of their duties. Lectures are given to be sure, but more exotic techniques are also used to sensitize trainees as to how they may be perceived. During handcuffing drills, students take turns handcuffing each other. Sometimes the handcuffs are left on for a long enough time so the students will appreciate the experience of being in custody and losing one's freedom of movement. In other exercises, students are exposed to pepper spray. While this is quickly washed off, they experience first-hand the effect of this widely used less-than-lethal weapon. To learn the dangers of a police state, students are taken on a tour of the Holocaust Museum in Washington, D.C.

The Training Schedule

Noting the caveat that the FBI is a changeable place, here is the allocation of training hours, as of early 2005:

Practical Exercises and Evaluation	86.5
Defensive Tactics/Arrest Techniques	78
Basic Investigative Techniques	136
Case Management	
Use of Criminal Informants, Intelligence	
Assets, and Cooperating Witnesses	
Background Investigations	
Civil Rights Investigations	
Weapons of Mass Destruction	
Firearms	114.5
Legal	77
Law Enforcement Communications	66
Forensic Science	36
Computer Training	31
Behavioral Science	8
Security Matters	5

National Crime Information Center   3
Drug Identification   2
Command Post Operations   2
Intelligence Orientation   2

          Total   647

Non-Investigative Matters   41.5
          (includes ethics training, cultural diversity,
          first aid, and various administrative
          lectures)

Administrative   13
          (includes graduation, oath of office,
          insurance matters, preparation of
          expense vouchers, and other
          administrative matters)

          Total   701.5

Why Some Don't Finish Training

Students sometimes depart the academy after a short time because they realize the role of FBI agent is not for them. These are particularly unfortunate losses to the training program, for they are completely avoidable. The applicant has frequent contacts with Special Agents during the recruiting, processing, and application process. These should have been used to explore fully the nature and requirements of the position. For a new agent to depart in training because he or she has finally come to the realization that FBI agents deal with people more than data is a needless loss for both the student and the Bureau.

Likewise, it's a loss when trainees have problems with the possibility of using deadly force. Most FBI agents go through a 20- or 25-year career without firing a shot in anger. Others do not. Nevertheless, the nature of the job may require the unavoidable use of deadly force. Those who have not considered this possibility should do so before they even begin the journey down the application path, thus saving themselves and the Bureau much wasted effort.

For example, the FBI has gone to substantial lengths to avoid situations such as these. Numerous discussions are held with the applicants. Pre-Quantico booklets and flyers are provided early on. There is even a free nine-minute video available on the FBI website that details the requirements of the agent position and the demands of the training program.

Some new agents are also lost because of poor test scores, be they in physical fitness, academics, or firearms. The FBI has a fair but firm policy about such matters, and it offers limited opportunities to take make-up tests, as noted above about the physical fitness test. However, the FBI is unrelenting in its application of these procedures, lest it be sued because it appeared to provide more assistance to one student than another.

Other students fail because of judgmental errors. These can be repeated failures in applying proper arrest techniques, interviewing procedures, or evidence collection protocols. A pattern of repeated firearms or safety violations is viewed seriously. Instructors are always nearby, and coaching is plentiful. However, every now and then, even after repeated attempts, some students simply "don't get it." Even then, one instructor cannot, on his or her own, wash a student out of the training program. What he or she can do is issue a written Notice of Counseling for any behavior or action that reflects negatively on a trainee. Additionally, a new agent may be counseled by his or her class supervisor. Written records are maintained of these counseling sessions, and the student is required to sign this document to acknowledge receipt of counseling.

Between the eight and tenth week of training, each new agent receives a mid-course review by the class supervisor or class counselor. The student's progress is discussed and remedial actions, if needed, are planned. The student is also asked to provide his or her thoughts on the training experience.

When a student is deficient in judgmental issues to the point that he is deemed unsuitable for the Special Agent position, a New Agents Review Board is convened. The board is headed by a unit chief and also has two Supervisory Special Agents, none of which can have been involved with or trained the student in question. The board hears evidence from instructors, classmates, and anyone else with pertinent information on the matter. The student can present testimony on behalf of himself and also call any witnesses he believes will advance his position. The Board then makes a recommendation to senior academy officials as to the appropriate disposition of the matter.

This same procedure is used in disciplinary cases, where a student has broken an academy rule or has had a run-in with the law outside of the academy. The most frequent mistake students make—which is investigated fully by the FBI—is to lie. Lack of candor is an automatic disqualifier and acts only to exacerbate an existing issue.

While the preceding portrays some of the less pleasant aspects of academy life, these are realistic situations and the message should be taken to heart. The FBI Academy does not function as some fictionalized flight training program, where a deliberate effort is made to eliminate a certain percentage of students. The FBI sincerely hopes all of its students make it through training, for a number of reasons. First, the FBI needs good people. Second, the FBI has invested considerable time and money in getting applicants to the stage at which they offer an appointment. Third, every student lost from the training program represents a slot that another equally deserving applicant could have held. Finally, there is the real, human element: the FBI is composed of people, and it does not like to see other people fail.

The FBI is also about some very serious business. The success of the FBI mission in years to come will depend on the quality of FBI agents who graduate from New Agents Training. And FBI agents are heavily armed, with powers of arrest. The FBI has an obligation to the public to put forth only the best, fully qualified agents it can, and so it is unrelenting in that mission. If this means some will fail or fall by the wayside, the Bureau is more than willing to pay that price. The FBI spends 65 percent of its budget on personnel—agents and support people—and it takes their development and qualifications very seriously.

The Field Assignment

As noted, week seven of the training cycle can be an important milestone for those who did not pass the physical fitness test in week one, but it is week six that is a time of peak interest for all class members. It is during week six that the new agents are informed of their first office of assignment. This is a radical departure from prior FBI practice. For decades, when the training cycle was 14 weeks long, office assignments were announced in week 11, shortly before graduation. The FBI realized, however, that in an era of two-career families and high housing costs in some areas, new agents and their families simply needed more time to adjust.

The process for office assignments is both simple and complex. Earlier in the training cycle, the new agent is asked to rank all 56 FBI field offices in order of preference. That is the simple part, but some try to game the system by anticipating the later stages of their careers.

There is a possible requirement in the FBI that all agents serve in a Top Fifteen office at an early stage of their careers. The FBI has vacillated on this issue over the years. Top Fifteen offices are determined by their population density, and they include New York City, Newark, Boston, Chicago, Los Angeles, Atlanta, Philadelphia, and a number of other cities. The rationale behind the FBI's policy is twofold: first, the Bureau believes the experience an agent gets working typically more complex investigations in a big office is valuable; second, since housing and living costs tend to be higher in big cities, this is an effort to spread the pain so that some do not suffer needlessly because of the luck of the draw.

In drawing up their preference lists, new agents use a variety of strategies. Some, originally from large cities, have no problem returning to them. Others, knowledgeable of the Bureau's requirement for Top Fifteen service, decide to get it out of the way while they are still single, or married without children, thereby planning for a transfer to a lower-cost area later in their careers when their housing needs will be greater. Still others want the excitement of a big-city environment and the chance to work on big cases that they believe will be career enhancing. Finally, some list only smaller offices at the top of their list, hoping they will get lucky and then deal with the Top Fifteen issue down the road.

At times, the system works fairly well, since on average new agents get about their fifth preference out of a possible 56. In some classes this average has been as high as third preference and in others it has been much lower. These differentials are due to a number of factors. For example, FBI Headquarters could have decided to substantially increase the staffing levels of one or more field offices; a new threat could have emerged in an area that was previously quiet; Congress could have provided funding for a new program or initiative; or a given field office could have been hit with a wave of unexpected retirements. Receiving these assignments in their sixth week of training allows new agents the time for houses to be sold, spouses to begin job searches, and children to be prepared for a move.

Weapons Training

Weapons are very common at Quantico, and they are taken very seriously. Whether it is a trainee or an experienced agent back for in-service training, a person never has a weapon or live ammunition in his or her possession at the academy. Weapons are checked into a gun vault (technically, the Weapons Maintenance Facility) and checked out when needed for a training exercise. They are then cleaned and returned to the gun vault. Obviously, experienced agents coming to the academy bring their weapons with them. These, too, are checked into the gun vault.

New agents have their weapons issued to them at the appropriate stage of the training cycle. On the wall opposite the Weapons Maintenance Facility there is a long display of the names of members of the "Possible" Club. These are agents and law-enforcement officers who have fired perfect scores during firearms training. Though ten of thousands of agents and law-enforcement officers have passed through Quantico since it opened, there are only several hundred names on the display.

New agent classes vary greatly in terms of exposure to firearms. Some trainees have come out of the military or law enforcement, and so will have great familiarity with firearms. Others never have fired a weapon in their lives. The differences in experience are unimportant. The firearms instructors at the academy have over a hundred years' cumulative experience in firearms training and can teach almost anyone to shoot. This is an important point to remember, since every now and then a trainee will, at his or her own expense and on his or her own time, undertake firearms instruction at a civilian facility prior to coming to Quantico in the belief that this will provide a leg up in the training cycle. This is time and money wasted and, indeed, may actually hurt the firearms training, since the FBI has its own style of firearms usage. It is true that from time to time a trainee flunks out owing to a lack of proficiency in firearms, but this is relatively rare. The trainee is best advised to put his or her faith in the professionalism of the firearms training staff.

Occasionally, a trainee who is doing well in other ways but having problems with firearms training will be recycled to a later training class. This is done to allow additional time to develop the necessary strength and skill to complete the firearms requirement. The trainee will be closely observed by the firearms training staff, and if the individual does not show rapid improvement, he or she may be recommended for dismissal.

To pass the firearms stage of training, the new agent must qualify twice with the Bureau-issued handgun and once with the shotgun. To qualify, the new agent must shoot 80 percent or better on two of the three pistol qualification courses, as well as a cumulative score of 80 percent on all three qualification courses. The new agent must also demonstrate familiarity with the Bureau submachine gun.

During the 18 weeks that new agents are in training at Quantico, they each fire between 3,000 and 5,000 rounds of ammunition. Because of the substantial amount of shooting in the training cycle, new agents are required to register all prescription drugs they may be taking with the Health Services Office and also inform their class supervisor and principal firearms instructor.

Practical Exercises

Those who closely scrutinize the hours distribution of the training cycle given earlier in the chapter may wonder what the 86.5 hours for Practical Exercises and Evaluation are all about. Many of these hours will be spent in the worst town in the United States, located just off the main campus. Hogan's Alley is a full-size small town, with shops, stores, a bank, a movie theater, a motel, a slum, and not a few really bad actors. On any given day, you may observe a group of new agents processing a car in a motel parking lot. Under the watchful eyes of their instructors, they dust for fingerprints, take copious notes and photographs, and collect evidence. Around the corner, in a seedy rooming house, another team of new agents are involved in a fierce gunfight with one or more desperados who have decided they would rather fight than be arrested. Again, FBI instructors closely monitor the exchange of nearly real gunfire, as Simunition rounds—actually hard plastic bullets—are fired at 400 feet per second from real weapons. Orange or blue in color, the rounds leave telltale smudges when they hit, and they sting a lot when they hit you.

Just down the block, another team of new agents is effecting a car stop, complete with lights and sirens. As the bad guys wait in their vehicle, the trainees, weapons drawn, issue commands to them over loudspeakers and advance slowly, crouched behind ballistic shields, to effect the arrest. Observing, again in abundant presence, are FBI instructors.

Back in the motel, whose parking lot is the scene of the car search, another team of new agents is using a functional motel room to set up a consensual monitoring station, from which they can observe and record an undercover buy in an adjacent room. Down the hall, yet another team of trainees is processing another motel room for evidence left by a group of terrorists who checked out earlier in the day. Again, instructors watch carefully and offer copious advice.

What makes Hogan's Alley function, other than the FBI experience and planning that went into its design and operation, are the role players. These are professionals, provided by an outside company under contract to the FBI. The actors, in the course of a week, get searched, arrested, interrogated, and sometimes "killed," only to come back and do it again next week. They have done this many times and have an inherent advantage. The new agents are doing it for the first time. The role players follow scripts, but they are also in radio contact with FBI instructors, who can modify a scenario to counter what the new agents are doing to see how they will react to real-life changes in circumstances. You would be correct to assume that the role players have many amusing incidents to recount to friends and family about the misadventures of the trainees.

If one were to talk to any old-time agent, he would likely recount some amusing anecdotes about his first arrest. Mistakes, thankfully few of them serious, were not uncommon then. FBI training has advanced a lot since the old days, and the purpose of the Practical Exercise and Evaluation portion is to have as many of them occur with role players and plastic bullets before the bad guys and the bullets become real.

The Integrated Case

In the recent past, the FBI introduced a new element into the training—the integrated case concept. This is a "real" FBI case, modeled after actual investigations that will "trail" the new agents during their entire training cycle. It is timed to coincide with various blocks of instruction, and it culminates in a "trial" in which the new agents will testify. Thus, when trainees are taught interview techniques and skills early on in their training, they also conduct and memorialize actual interviews. These are later used at the "trial" and the new agents may have to testify to their interview results. So, too, for evidence collection, when the completeness and adequacy of their ability to complete the evidence cycle— identify, collect, preserve, and analyze—is tested in a courtroom setting with FBI lawyers hammering them as "defense counsel." Even arrests and searches at the notorious Hogan's Alley come into play in the integrated case, as does surveillance activities.

The idea is to give new agents experience with the various elements that go into the making of an actual case and also provide familiarity with the stringent demands of the U.S. legal system in trial proceedings. In real life the trainees will be new FBI agents, working real cases and going up against some smart and experienced defense counsels. Even with the assistance of experienced and dedicated assistant U.S. attorneys, they will be tested in the real world, and they must pass.

From Graduation to Retirement

Thus, in some granularity, this is how almost 18 weeks at Quantico is spent. Believe it or not, the time flies by. After a few days' residence you quickly fall into the rhythm of the place. The days are full, but each is an adventure, with you being exposed to new material and new challenges. The instructors are knowledgeable, helpful, and often funny. They, too, are full of war stories from their FBI careers and not much is required to get the "I remember once" valve to open. Fellow students, given their variety of backgrounds and career accomplishments, are also a source of wonder. When you have a former Air Force command pilot, college professor, and investment banker involved in a conversation, it can get interesting. Parties happen, as do group trips to Washington, D.C., or Richmond. You are around some pretty neat people. And it is just not FBI all the time. After your study group breaks up in the evening, a trip to The Boardroom, the on-campus pub, can involve sitting around a table sharing a beer with a major-city chief of police, in for a conference; a sheriff from an area that still does patrols on horseback; a police executive from Asia; and a veteran homicide detective with over a hundred investigations to their credit. Again, folks you do not meet every day.

There are, however, significant limits on the amount of social interaction in after-hours settings. At any one time there are multiple classes of new agents going through the training cycle. You may be tempted to ask someone from a class further along in the cycle for assistance regarding tests or practical problem exercises. The FBI Academy strictly forbids a range of behavior in this arena, to include receiving or giving exam questions or answers; sharing classroom notes; passing papers that have been graded or returned for review; discussing exams, practical problems, or any other matter subject to being graded; willfully furnishing false or inaccurate information to an academy instructor; and obtaining or using the work product of another.

The often emotional highlight of New Agents Training is that point in the graduation ceremony when the new agent walks across the auditorium stage, with family and friends in attendance and cameras flashing, to receive his or her credentials. Sometimes these are presented by the director and other times by the assistant director in charge of the Training Division. In the famous movie *The Silence of the Lambs*, a little known fact is that actress Jodie Foster, playing Agent Clarice Starling, received her "credentials" from the real assistant director of the FBI Academy at the time, Tony Daniels. Other real academy officials were also on stage.

FBI credentials, carried folded over, measure about 5 inches by 6 inches when opened. Nearly all agents carry them in a leather case with a flap on the front and a clip on the back. The clip allows the credentials to be secured in a jacket pocket, usually the right inside breast pocket of a suit coat. This is done for a very practical reason. Most people are right-handed, so when it is necessary to display their credentials, most agents reach for them with their left hands. This leaves the gun hand free in case it turns out that the person to whom they are being displayed is a potential adversary.

The flap on the front of the credential case has a carved-out area to accommodate the Special Agent badge. Just below the badge, on the back side of the flap, is a Velcro strip that keeps the badge flush against the credential case. When an agent needs to have the badge displayed for a long time, such as when working on a crime scene, the flap can be opened and the credential case secured in an outside coat pocket. This allows the badge to hang free on the flap, secured by the body of the credential case in the pocket.

Agents can become very ritualistic about their credentials. They know where they are at all times. Many old-time agents develop a kind of "pat down" procedure they go through before leaving their residence each morning, touching various parts of their bodies to make sure they have everything—credentials, weapon, ammunition, handcuffs, and car keys. When an agent retires, his or her credentials, badge, and service keys are mounted by the Bureau on a wooden plaque and presented at the retirement ceremony. The credentials have been stamped "Retired," but they will invariably receive a place of honor in the agent's home. Oftentimes, when a retired agent dies, the retirement plaque and credentials are placed at the head of the coffin.

In 2005, the director of the FBI authorized the issuance of "retired" credentials to former Special Agents and other FBI employees who had served a minimum number of years and had departed in good standing. These credentials have no immediate function other than to recognize the agent's service, but they may come into play if the concept of an FBI Reserve Force, discussed after the events of 9/11, ever comes to fruition.

Conclusion

An agent leaves the FBI Academy a changed person in many ways. Even though the experience is somewhat collegiate in nature, with a lot of shooting thrown in, the regimen is tough. As with the military and athletic programs, there is a premium on teamwork, as strangers thrown together by fate become a cohesive whole. Friendships form and trust develops. Accordingly, whether you stay in the FBI but a few years or several decades, it is not uncommon to remain in touch with one or more of your training classmates for decades to come, or even an entire lifetime. The bonds are deep, the memories are good, and there are always war stories to share.

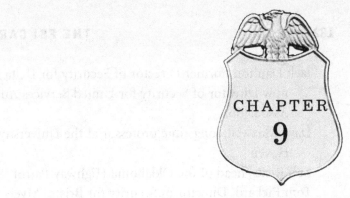

Life After the Bureau

One could construct an interesting parlor game around the following questions: What do the following persons have in common?

Frank Keating, former Governor of Oklahoma

Don Edwards, former Congressman from California

Mike Oxley, Congressman from Ohio, head of the House
Financial Services Committee, and co-author of the famous
Sarbanes-Oxley Act

Bill Baker, former President of the Motion Picture Association of
America

Joe Wells, founder and Chairman Emeritus of the 33,000-member
Association of Certified Fraud Examiners, and several times
included in the list of the 100 Most Influential People in
Accounting

Robert Strauss, former Chairman of the Democratic National
Committee and previous U.S. Ambassador to the Soviet
Union

Milt Ahlerich, Director of Security of the National Football League

Tom Sheer, former Executive Director of the U.S. Knights of
Malta

Jack Daulton, former Director of Security for Delta Airlines and
    now Director of Security for United Services Automobile
    Association
Dave Maxwell, long-time professor at the University of New
    Haven
Bob Ricks, head of the Oklahoma Highway Patrol
Tom Pickard, Director of Security for Bristol Myers Squibb
Kevin Donovan, Director of Security for Johnson & Johnson
Ken Maxwell, Director of Security for JetBlue Airlines
Roger Viadero, former Inspector General of the U.S. Department
    of Agriculture

They are all former FBI agents. Some served for but a few years while
others completed full careers. That they all share the common background of having been agents may be somewhat less than coincidence.

This chapter explores the myriad ways experience as an FBI agent
prepares one for the private sector and other careers.

The Reputation Precedes You

As noted at the beginning of this book, the FBI sometimes functions
as a brand. To some degree, the issue of brand carries over to FBI
agents as well, even after they leave the Bureau. There is no substitute
for imagination, ambition, intelligence, hard work and perseverance,
but carrying the FBI brand, or image, forward with you often does
not hurt. Why this is so may be a function of halo effect or mythology
about the FBI. Some people are fascinated by the organization, its
deeds and history, and its Special Agents. Other factors may, however,
also come into play.

While FBI agents are not perfect, they have been through a career-
long process of selection and evaluation that began with their initial
selection. These processes, from the first day until the last year, tend
to weed out people who are grossly deficient. Those who survive are
usually worthy of serious consideration.

The FBI is tough to get into. It seeks intelligent, fit, ambitious, accomplished, personable, and hardworking people; it trains them well, works them hard, and confronts them with incredible professional challenges. In the course of doing this, the FBI seeks, teaches, and promotes many skills, a fair number of which carry well into the private sector. Among these are:

• *The ability to analyze and prioritize.* Beginning a major criminal investigation is like assembling a complex jigsaw puzzle that is made out of ice. The task is daunting enough, but you do not have all day. Evidence disappears, memories dim, rain may wash away a crime scene, and witnesses may begin to compare notes and amend their stories. Accordingly, an agent must quickly assess the facts of a situation, decide what is most important, evaluate the resources at his or her disposal, and make decisions as to what gets done, in what order, and by whom.

• *The ability to make decisions.* Law enforcement does not offer many opportunities for indecision. The need for sound, rapid decisions are legion: shoot or don't shoot; arrest or let go; seize potential evidence now or wait until later when there may be more; begin a foot or vehicle chase or try to get the bad guy later; ask the key question now or wait for a more opportune time; accept what an informant has to offer or try to get a better source; pay informant X for useful information or try to get a better deal; insert an undercover agent into a dangerous situation or not. In a dynamic, fast-paced, competitive world, the ability to make rapid, informed, and correct decisions gives an edge in any number of fields.

• *Good people skills.* Much of the work of an agent involves data gathering. Some of this is from databases and records systems, but the vast majority of it comes from people. Informants, witnesses, prosecutors, suspects, friends and relatives of fugitives, scared victims, and many others share one trait. They are people. The ability to deal with people from a great variety of backgrounds with varying interests and agendas, perhaps only having fragments of useful information, sometimes trying to conceal what they have, and potentially trying to find out how much you already know, is a valuable skill. The skill to deal with people and successfully elicit information and cooperation from them is perhaps the single greatest predictor of success as an agent. These dealings may involve elements of cajoling, flattery, probing, negotiation, intimidation, deception, and the reading of nonverbal clues, but they are vital—in law enforcement as in much else of life. And these transactions will take place with people from all walks of life and many different cultures. An FBI agent may literally be talking to the president of a major corporation and a crack-addicted prostitute in the space of several hours on the same day.

• *A knowledge of risk, vulnerability, and criminal behavior.* After a number of years as a criminal investigator, you begin to understand "the street," criminal scams and conduct, institutional weaknesses that can be exploited by criminals, deterrent strategies, and potential risk. You can view an ordinary business situation, whether it be a financial transaction or a stocked warehouse, from the perspective of a criminal seeking to exploit that opportunity for personal interests. The experienced investigator can anticipate how criminals see the world and react to situations. You also gain an appreciation for "street justice," the code that operates even in nether regions of the underworld. These heightened sensitivities allow the agent moving into the world of corporate security to do a much better job assisting the employer in defending itself against likely attack. It is a valuable skill.

• *Knowledge of the criminal justice system.* There are almost 17,000 law-enforcement agencies in the United States. And this does not count prosecutors, courts, juvenile programs, prisons, parole offices, or other elements of the criminal justice system. They can have much in common and at the same time be incredibly diverse. Understanding how they operate, what their missions and priorities are, who their key personnel are, and perhaps most important, how to deal with them is an invaluable asset. Many former agents in corporate security positions have dealings with law-enforcement agencies on a weekly or even daily basis. Understanding how to mesh the needs of their employers with the interests of the criminal justice agency can better serve the needs of the company or corporation.

• *Good planning and organizational skills.* FBI agents rarely work alone. Whether operating with one partner or as part of a large task force, agents must not only plan and coordinate their own work but also that of others. In the case of a large, complex investigation, that work may entail formulating and executing a game plan involving a dozen or more people. In truly huge investigations, as of the crash of TWA flight 800 into Long Island Sound, there were over 1,000 agents assigned to the inquiry. Certainly, executive, senior, and mid-level managers played a large role in coordinating and directing this work, but these organizational responsibilities also fell on street agents working the investigation. Such experience and ability translate well to the private sector, since work in many fields requires the coordinated efforts of a number of people.

• *The ability to collect information.* As noted earlier, an investigator is mainly a collector of information. Frequently, this skill comes into play in dealing with people, but a highly competent agent is adept at seeking out numerous sources of alternative data. These sources may be official or corporate records, regulatory filings, court documents, census records, or financial profiles. Such information sources are not uncommon at crime scenes, either, and creativity here can pay handsome dividends. For example, at a mob hit at a mid-town Manhattan restaurant, experienced homicide investigators immediately collected all credit card receipts from the cash register and also took the license numbers of vehicles parked in a two-block radius of the establishment. Their theory was that patrons who had already paid may have lingered over coffee, saw the murder, and fled in panic immediately thereafter. Likewise, someone may have instinctively run down the street or hailed a cab instead of taking the time to return to a parked car. The ability to be creative and persistent in seeking out data often spells the difference between investigative success and failure. Such is also true in the corporate world after the Bureau.

• *Good time-management skills.* The judicial system in the United States is a thing of deadlines. Trial and hearing dates are set and are absolute. Statutes of limitations have set legal lifetimes. The quality and quantity of evidence deteriorates rapidly with age. All of these factors require that a competent agent be an excellent manager of time. So, too, with the agent's own time. A busy agent may have been assigned multiple investigative matters and also have responsibilities for training activities, family obligations, and other activities as well. The ability to manage time productively is essential to success.

• *The ability to function under pressure.* As the discussion of time management above indicates, pressure comes with the job. The ability to function well in a demanding, ever-changing, high-stress environment is vital to success. Dealing with these pressures is one of the reasons that time management and teamwork are so important. There is a need to get the job done, get it right, and finish it on time. Often there are competing interests between agencies, between investigators and prosecutors, between the government and the media, between squads or programs in the same field office, and even between investigators working on the same case. Human dynamics play a great role, as well. Criminals by definition are not nice people and many informants or cooperating witnesses may not be, as well. Functioning in such an environment can be a testing experience, but at the same time it produces skills that will be useful throughout your professional life.

• *The ability to make a point.* FBI agents, by definition, are gatherers of information. However, their task does not stop there. They need to be able to organize and present that information in a manner that is factual, persuasive, and concise. Whether seeking authorization for a search warrant from an Assistant U.S. Attorney, testifying before a jury, or arguing for a budget increase in an FBI program, agents must be able to present their case in a professional, persuasive manner. Oral and written communications skills are vital to success. Obviously, these skills transfer well to the private sector, where such demands are common.

• *The ability to show discretion.* All FBI agents hold a top secret clearance throughout their careers, even if they work solely on criminal investigations. Some agents assigned to intelligence and terrorism matters may hold additional clearances. All agents, regardless of their duties, have daily access to highly sensitive and even potentially dangerous information, be it about drug dealing, criminal informants, or political corruption. The ability to securely handle such information as a matter of course is also valuable to a corporation, whose most sensitive inner secrets may be in the hands of a director of security.

• *The ability to use international experience and contacts.* As noted, the FBI is increasingly becoming an international entity, as it responds to terrorism, drug cartels, and organized criminal enterprises on a worldwide basis. So, too, has corporate America become international, to the point that many U.S. corporations make over half their profits from foreign operations. The ability of a former agent to operate overseas, with knowledge of local laws and protocols, and contacts with foreign government officials, makes the candidate very attractive to prospective employers.

• *The ability to do quality work.* The work of an agent is often subject to inspection and review in one of the world's toughest forums: a courtroom. Prosecutors, judges, juries, defense counsels, and appellate courts examine every word, question every assumption, and challenge every procedure undertaken or not pursued. To put it simply, the work has to be right—every time, all the time. Review can also come from superiors in the FBI field office, from FBI Headquarters, and from the FBI inspection staff. If the matter gains the attention of the media, any number of pundits and talking heads can be expected to opine, fairly or otherwise, on what was done or not done. The ability to produce quality work under pressure is valuable in any field.

• *The ability to show courage.* It may seem redundant to mention courage as a skill of an FBI agent, but courage takes many forms. Certainly, the physical courage to face an armed opponent comes to mind, but there are many other instances when it comes into play. Emotional and psychological courage is needed when dealing with a mob hit man in a contentious interview. Intellectual and moral courage appears when arguing with a prosecutor for a given course of action in an investigation. Tactical and procedural courage is used when defending your work during an inspection that challenges how you could or should have pursued an investigation. Moral courage is always at a premium in a criminal world where bribes, sexual favors, and graft are the coin of the realm. The power of your convictions is vital to function in any complex, demanding environment, be it public or private.

Retirement Choices

Lest you think that former agents wind up only in white-collar, executive positions, understand that nothing could be further from the truth. Former agents find a wide variety of postretirement livelihoods and avocations, to include ranching, teaching, church work, innkeeping, being a disk jockey, doing animal rescue work, offering skiing instruction, being a saloon owner, offering private investment counseling, piloting airplanes, developing a small business, becoming a politician, captaining a commercial fishing boat, and much more. Some use their long experience and contacts in law enforcement to move into state or local agencies, usually in some executive position. Others become affiliated with international training programs of the U.S. government and spend several months a year in foreign countries, instructing their foreign counterparts in bomb detection, public corruption, organized crime, counterterrorism operations, and much more.

Some former agents also choose to get private investigator licenses in one or more states. Considering their credentials, this is fairly simple, and allows the agent to conduct private investigations for persons and corporate clients.

Like their active-duty brethren, retired agents also act as mentors to young people interested in careers in law enforcement in general and in the FBI in particular. They may do this informally, through family, relatives, neighbors, and friends, or more formally, as when involved with a local college or university. Also, like active-duty agents, they find themselves dispensing innumerable pieces of gear bearing the FBI seal or name.

Cautions for the Newly Retired

FBI agents generally retire at about age 50, with 20 or more years of service, and they tend to be in good physical shape. Though many launch full second careers, others prefer to maintain a semi-retired status, performing occasional investigative or consulting assignments.

Some former agents are quite visible. Any time there is a major criminal or terrorism incident around the world, you can see them on television. They are the talking heads of current television production. They may be commenting on terrorism issues, serial killings, high-profile trials, or unsolved cases—but they are talking. Other former agents write books, talking about themselves, what they found right or wrong with the FBI during their careers, or how they see current battles against terrorism, drug cartels, or child abuse. Some also appear as expert witnesses in criminal and civil trials

Still others write books about their careers and experiences. For those who do, there is a federal requirement that applies to all former federal employees who held sensitive security clearances. The manuscript of the book must be submitted to FBI Headquarters for prepublication review, regardless of its subject matter or content. The intent is to avoid the former agent's intentionally or inadvertently revealing classified or sensitive information. Generally, this is not a problem, although there have been instances in which former agents and the Bureau got into heated disagreement as to what was sensitive or inappropriate. In requiring this procedure, the FBI is quite fair. If the book is critical of the FBI or some of its current or former employees, that is not a problem. The FBI is used to criticism, no matter how much it might not like it. The issue of sensitive information, however, concerns the Bureau greatly.

In addition to the workplace skills and attributes discussed above, social interaction and networking are also part of the agent's world. These are valuable sources of support and information while on the job and they become even more so after an agent leaves the Bureau. In brief, agents like to help each other. They frequently refer job leads to each other, hire each other as deputies and subcontractors, and share information on private sector job matters. The ability to resolve a vexing corporate problem with a phone call to a former colleague saves valuable time and resources, and makes the decision to hire a former agent look like an excellent investment.

A word of caution, however. Once you leave the FBI, an invisible but very important line has been crossed. Certainly, you know agents who are still active within the Bureau and also any number of former associates still active in other law-enforcement agencies. There may from time to time be a temptation to reach back to these people to inquire about the status of an investigation of interest to your current employer. But there is no action so potentially damaging and dangerous as gaining access to something you should not have access to, regardless of the depth of your personal friendship. Once you are out of active service, you are out forever. Only bad things can come from delving into an active investigation or trying to influence its outcome.

Pension and Other Benefits at Retirement

Agents retire with government pensions that are a function of their years of service and the average of their three highest years' salaries. Depending on a number of factors, agent pensions at this time are in the $65,000 to $85,000 range. Those retiring from the Senior Executive Service can have pensions that are considerably higher. Some retired agents, because of their family circumstances or professional ambitions, continue to work after retirement. A few are even able to bank their retirement money and live off of their new salary, creating a nice nest egg over the years. Others choose to give up active employment to spend time with family and friends, travel, or pursue civic activities.

Agents may, at the time of their retirement, make a one-time decision to forgo a portion of their retirement money in exchange for a spousal annuity. This means that at the time of the retired agent's death, the spouse will receive about 65 percent of the agent's retirement for as long as the spouse lives, even if he or she chooses to remarry. No matter what decisions an agent makes regarding retirement, the retirement benefit (which is adjusted for inflation annually) permits a range of options not every American worker enjoys.

In 2004, the Congress passed, and the president signed, House Resolution 218, which among other things allows former federal agents who served a designated minimum amount of time and left their agencies in good standing to apply for permits to carry a concealed weapon in their home states. It is important to note that this is not a federal authority, but rather an inducement for various states to afford this option to former agents and others. There are training and identification requirements attached to the legislation, which as of 2005 is still in the process of being implemented. As a result of this legislation, in 2005 the director of the FBI authorized the FBI to issue "retired" credentials to former Special Agents who meet certain criteria. The processing of these requests began in FBI field offices in May 2005, and it requires the retired agent to pay a $75 processing fee and also appear at the field office for a photograph and other administrative processing.

The Post-Retirement Family

While much networking is informal, there is one formal mechanism to promote it: the Society of Former Special Agents of the FBI. Founded in 1937, the society has about 8,000 members. Membership is open to any agent who left the FBI in good standing. *The Grapevine* is the monthly magazine of the society, and it publishes articles of interest, chapter and national news, lists of scholarship awards, and death and illness announcements. The society also offers scholarships, family assistance, investment advice, and bereavement assistance, and it is very good at getting the word out when a member is ill or has passed away.

Membership does not end with death, as odd as that might sound. Spouses are considered to be members of the FBI family, and the society goes out of its way to include them in activities and post news of significant events in their lives. In cases of financial hardship, the society has been known to help out in a quiet, discrete, and dignified way.

In most cities where there is a society chapter, there are monthly lunches with guest speakers from the community, the worlds of sports and politics, or prominent members of area law enforcement. Often, in addition to the monthly lunches, there are fishing trips, golf outings, and other social events. The society also sponsors both regional and national conferences on a yearly basis.

In addition to the work of the society, there are numerous informal groups of former agents who get together for class and squad reunions, and who generally stay in touch. Some go into business with each other while others limit their associations to lunches, golf, and fishing. There are numerous professional organizations that former agents also join, either while on active duty or in retirement. These associations offer companionship, job leads, and professional development activities. Some of the more prominent are:

• *American Society for Industrial Security.* This 33,000-member organization has been in existence since 1955 and is worldwide in scope. Most security professionals in the private sector belong to it, as do many persons still active in law enforcement. The group offers training, certification as a Certified Protection Professional, and social, job development, and seminar activities throughout the year and

around the world. The annual convention draws in excess of 10,000
members, vendors, and persons interested in the corporate security
field. Numerous committees within the group are formed around the
security interests of various industry groups, such as retail, gaming,
hotels, transportation, educational institutions, financial institutions,
or energy.

• *International Security Management Association.* This group
has fewer than 500 members and comprises the top corporate security
professionals in the world. Membership is limited to only the top security personnel in major corporations and a select number of vendors of security and security-related products. The group offers
professional development, social, and networking services. Members
use each other, via an Internet link, to research issues and opportunities of interest to the companies for which they work. This group also
functions as somewhat of a discreet hiring hall, for its members tend
to have the inside word on the top security jobs available in the private
sector.

• *Association of Certified Fraud Examiners.* This 32,000-member
worldwide group is composed of persons in the public and private
sectors with an interest in fraud detection and deterrence. Founded in
1988, its many members are auditors, academics, and forensic accountants. The leading organization of its type in the world, it offers certification as a Certified Fraud Examiner and also provides social,
training, and seminar activities. Its annual convention has in excess of
1,000 attendees. The association has, over the years, had an uncanny
ability to attract national convention speakers who have participated
in some of the most significant corporate frauds of recent years, thus
enabling members in attendance to hear from the speakers—some
fresh out of prison—as to how they actually "did it" and how they
got caught.

• *International Association of Chiefs of Police.* This 19,000-
member organization was founded in 1893 and has members in
almost 100 countries. It is composed of persons active in law enforce-

ment, former law-enforcement officials, academics, and others interested in the law-enforcement community, such as vendors. Training, social, and seminar activities are offered throughout the year. The annual convention draws in excess of 15,000 attendees, be they members, vendors, or persons interested in law enforcement.

• *Police Executive Research Forum.* This 1,100-member group was founded in 1976 and is devoted to cutting-edge issues in law enforcement, legislation, and research. Members are normally heads or high-ranking members of their agencies, retired executives, and academics.

• *Association of Former Intelligence Officers.* This 4,500-member group was formed in 1975 and is composed of active and former intelligence officers, academics, and persons with an interest in intelligence activities. A large portion of the membership is military. The group offers social, research, networking, and job services activities.

• *FBI National Academy Associates.* This group has in excess of 17,000 members, all of whom are graduates of the FBI National Academy training program. Agents who served as counselors to that program are also eligible for membership. The group holds periodic training sessions for those still active in law enforcement and offers an array of social, sporting, and other activities. There are chapters in most cities and regions of the country, and most foreign countries. Usually, any active-duty or former agent is also welcome to join in these functions, whether they were an academy counselor or not.

• *Police Benevolent Association (PBA) Local 121.* The PBA is an old and well-established law-enforcement organization that primarily represents the interests of uniformed law-enforcement personnel. In addition to providing social and professional services and benefits, in some areas it functions as a union, representing the interests of its members in contract negotiations and personnel matters. Local 121 is unique, in that it is composed entirely of federal agents, both active and retired. Some former agents choose to join it for social and professional reasons.

Trapline is a reference guide that has been run by a former agent for many years. For a modest annual fee, former agents interested in performing investigative services, consultative work, expert witness testimony, or document and fingerprint examinations can list their availability. There are about 40 categories of expertise to self-select. *Trapline* is available only to other former agents, but it provides a quick reference guide when seeking a specific expertise or when looking for investigative assistance in another part of the country.

The Commission on Accreditation of Law Enforcement Agencies (CALEA) is an independent group that includes a number of former FBI agents and senior executives. It was formed in 1979, at the direction of four longstanding law-enforcement organizations: the International Association of Chiefs of Police, the National Organization of Black Law Enforcement Executives (NOBLE), the National Sheriff's Association, and the Police Executive Research Foundation. For a fee, this group will inspect a law-enforcement agency against a set of leading practice standards and either issue it a certification or work with the organization to address operational or procedural deficiencies.

There is even an FBI chat room, hosted by a retired agent, where former agents and others trade news, gossip, political gripes, thoughts about the FBI, past and present, and general items of interest.

We are Family

Family: that is perhaps the best word to describe the FBI experience, active or retired. The group functions much like a family, with all the pluses and minuses that pertain to family relationships. New agents will be entering a world where they will—knowingly or not—acquire brothers and sisters who will be additions to their biological family. You will come to care about many of these people. New Agents Training is a special time when all are "promoted" to the rank of rookie, regardless of credentials and background. New agents will be exposed to training and challenges known to very few of their fellow citizens. They will be challenged and they will grow as these challenges are met.

They will come to realize that *success* is a plural word, and that very little is done in law enforcement that is not a team effort. They will come to understand that having confidence in a fellow agent may mean the difference between life and death, and also come to the realization that others look to them in the same manner. They will trust strangers on the basis that they, too, are "agents."

The process continues and intensifies in the field office, where your very survival can depend on the competence and courage of your peers. It has been said that there are no atheists in a foxhole. Service as an FBI agent is not combat, but it is very different from what most people experience in their professional and personal lives. Many times outsiders are amazed at the number of active and former agents who turn out for an agent's funeral, be the deceased active or retired. Often outsiders comment, wistfully, to the effect that "You guys really stick together, don't you?"

Yes, we do. We attend birthdays, weddings, funerals, and much more. We call on former colleagues who are sick. We spent many years in a special world, doing special things. We care about each other. It is complex and simple at the same time. In the FBI experience, there is support, friendship, assistance and caring, and there are squabbles, cliques, and disputes. The overarching theme, however, is that all agents—active, resigned, or retired—have shared the distinction of carrying the credentials of an FBI agent. They are all in the business of service to their country and living life together. *Together* here is the operative word. There are very few loners in the FBI.

It is more than a job. It demands more and it gives more. It is not for everyone. For those who choose it (and are chosen), few regret the decision. It is a job, with all the pluses and minuses that entails, but at its core it is a love affair. I hope you make the right choice. It will be a part of you forever.

Index

About the Author

Joe Koletar is a 25-year veteran of the FBI, having served as a Special Agent, Supervisory Special Agent, Headquarters Supervisor, Unit Chief, Assistant Section Chief, Inspector, Assistant Special Agent in Charge, Special Agent in Charge, and Section Chief. He has conducted and supervised over 1,000 criminal investigations and testified in over 50 judicial proceedings. He was in charge of all applicant recruiting and testing for the FBI's largest field office, New York City. He holds a bachelor's degree from the Pennsylvania State University, a master's degree from George Washington University, and both master's and doctoral degrees from the University of Southern California. He is also a graduate of the Program for Senior Managers in Government at Harvard University and the Senior Executive Officers Course at the Australian Police Staff College.

As an associate of the Advisory Board for the Crime, Law and Justice Program at Penn State, Koletar has dealt for many years with students interested in law-enforcement careers. His previous book, *Fraud Exposed: What You Don't Know Could Cost Your Company Millions*, was published by John Wiley & Sons in 2003. He is also the author of three sections in the *Encyclopedia of Law Enforcement* (Thousand Oaks, Calif.: Sage Publications, 2004).

Look for These Exciting Career Titles at
www.amacombooks.org/careers

The Career Troubleshooter by Sherrie Gong Taguchi $14.95

Cracking the Corporate Code by Price M. Cobbs and Judith L. Turnock $24.95

The Elements of Résumé Style by Scott Bennett $9.95

The Etiquette Edge by Beverly Langford $14.95

The Girls' Guide to Power and Success by Susan Wilson Solovic $14.00

The Job Search Solution by Tony Beshara $16.95

Make Your Contacts Count by Anne Baber and Lynne Waymon $14.95

The Portable Mentor by Cy Charney $18.95

The Power of Charm by Brian Tracy and Ron Arden $15.00

Power Etiquette by Dana May Casperson $15.95

Suite Success by Liza Siegel, Ph.D. $19.95

The Virtual Handshake by David Teten and Scott Allen $19.95

Why Men Earn More by Warren Farrell, Ph.D. $23.00

Winning the Interview Game by Alan H. Nierenberg $12.95

Writing for Quick Cash by Loriann Hoff Oberlin $14.95

Your Successful Real Estate Career, Fourth Edition, by Kenneth W. Edwards $18.95
